I MAKE A DIFFERENCE

A Process to Heal and Dissolve the Layers from Your Past and Discover the Jewel Within

Melinda Cates

www.imakeadifferenceimad.com
www.melindacates.com

ISBN Kindle: 978-0-473-47576-5
ISBN iBook: 978-0-473-47577-2
ISBN Softcover: 978-0-473-47574-1
ISBN Hardcover: 978-0-473-47575-8
ISBN Digital Audiobook: 978-0-473-48153-7

DOWNLOAD YOUR PERSONAL PROCESSING WORKBOOK

As you embark on your I Make a Difference adventure of internal exploration of yourself, you deserve to have a companion to journey with you—the I Make a Difference Personal Processing Workbook.

This workbook offers a convenient space for you to record your responses to the Self-Facilitation Activities provided in this book.

I want to give you this gift because you deserve it—access the I Make a Difference Personal Processing Workbook for free.

Visit http://bit.ly/imadppworkbook to download.

For the key people who helped me get to here:

Mum—I chose you as my mum. You are my city of jewels. You exposed me to as many dimensions of life as you could at the time. You loved me even though I scared you. You believed in me even when you felt powerless. You cared for me when you were struggling. You are MY MUM.

Alan—your love enabled me to accept I was lovable. Your love helped me heal my vulnerability and my fear of being left again. Your belief and knowing have held my hand in our journeys and experiences to get me to where I am now. We were meant to be. You are my one.

Yillie—my spiritual mum, my spiritual mentor, and my friend—your love is palpable. Your belief is the hope I felt. Without your words, without your wisdom, without your consistency of being, without your magnificence, I would not have found me.

Thank you—I love you guys.

CONTENTS

Foreword—Journey To The Jewel Within.................................vii

1 The True You..1

2 How I Became IMAD..15

3 Preparation for Your Adventure Inside: The I Make a Difference Onion Model...41

4 The IMAD Onion Model: The Creation of Your Layers............65

5 The IMAD Onion Model: Preserving Your Layers.................87

6 The IMAD Onion Model: Inside Your Layers.....................123

7 The IMAD Onion Model: The Last Line of Protection............151

8 Integration of You...173

9 Beliefs Within the Layers...201

10 Responding Rather Than Reacting................................245

11 More on the Five Steps..279

12 Lessons, Learnings, Uncovering, and Discovering Stages....305

13 You Make a Difference to Your Life..............................327

About The I Make A Difference Book Collection...................341

Acknowledgments..345

About The Author...349

JOURNEY TO THE JEWEL WITHIN

I remember a time, probably in my early twenties, where I was so caught up in my emotions, so caught up in what was happening to me, that I thought I was the only person in the world to ever experience this intensity.

I thought that no one could possibly understand what I was feeling—the thoughts I was thinking—or the actions I was taking, as a result of all these emotions.

I truly believed, as I'm sure you have experienced too, that I was somehow special, different, that I had somehow won some weird lottery in the Universe where I would be the only person who got to experience life as part of the School of Hard Knocks . . .

How crazy is that?

Yet, it does have a ring of truth to it—my truth. And it could be your truth too.

The thing is this—you and I are the same, but different. We might share the same experiences, but we experience them differently ...

In the summer of 2002, I was 24 and had just gone through an extremely emotional breakup with a guy I thought I was meant to spend the rest of my life with. I truly felt like my world was falling apart. To an extent, it was, but not in the way I thought.

I can't remember how I found out about Melinda Cates's I Make a Difference (IMAD) program, but I do remember entering the room on the introduction evening and immediately feeling a sense of peace and understanding.

Over the next few hours, two beautiful women Melinda and her then co-facilitator, Mere, guided me along with the other participants through some amazing journeys of self-discovery and enlightenment. So much so, that I knew I had to continue with the I Make a Difference process. Let me add—"process" is a word you'll see a lot in this book. It's a large part of what makes I Make a Difference so special.

It all started with the amazing and open-hearted IMAD founder, Melinda Cates, who you'll learn more about as you progress through this book. By deciding to share her own knowledge, experiences, and process (and processing) through the I Make a Difference program, Melinda has made a tangible difference in my life.

Back in 2002, that program was an intense three-day workshop. And it is, without a doubt, the most life-changing three days I've ever experienced in my life. And I'm still experiencing the learnings and understandings I received during that summer.

And I owe it all to Melinda.

She has since become a mentor and close friend, and has so much insight and genuinity about her that I know that you're going to get what you need from this book. And that's the crux of everything you're about to learn: your experience in reading this book will be vastly different to another person reading the very same words. And that's OK. It's your process, your processing, your journey.

I love this book because it will prompt you to explore areas inside yourself that you weren't even aware of, explore beliefs and thoughts you've always had, and provide you with a way of peeling back the layers to get to the real you—your jewel within.

Without a doubt, the Onion Model is my favorite part of the I Make a Difference process. You'll find out why in a very short time.

It's time for you to take a journey inside yourself and allow Melinda to guide you through this experience. I encourage you to read this book with an open mind and absorb everything you can.

I wish you well as you journey to the jewel within YOU and make a difference to yourself, your family, your friends, your colleagues, and our world.

Lise Cartwright, Author
Te Awamutu, New Zealand

CHAPTER 1

THE TRUE YOU

There is a place within you that is so pure, untouched by the outside world and is the essence of who you are. A space that is limitless, where the qualities and attributes that are you exist and emanate. Where all the answers you ever need for yourself reside. The home of your knowing, your truth and the unique, natural, and true you. This is the jewel within you.

So why do you only fleetingly feel it? Only occasionally see the light within yourself and doubt that it is you? Why is it that you struggle to trust yourself, believe in yourself, value, and know yourself?

However—you do know the real you.

There is a moment in time you will remember when inside yourself, you felt safe, free, and full of wonder, at peace, and filled with gentleness and love. A time when everything felt right in your world and all that mattered was what was in front of you and the joy you experienced. When you were you.

To remember and feel this experience means you are still connected to these parts of yourself, the true you. The person you were born as and truly are. The you that had light filling every single cell of your being as it shone through your eyes, your tone, your words, and what you did. When you were the jewel that is within you.

What happened?

Your likely response—"Life happened."

Yes, it did. Life, where suddenly who you truly are, did not fit in the world around you. Where the messages sent to you were ones of non-acceptance and rejection. And you started to doubt who you were, you started not trusting what was right for you, so you changed how you showed yourself to the world.

You had what I call a "layer experience," a term you will come to know well in this book, where you covered up and dimmed the light of the jewel within yourself. Slowly but surely you started losing the connection with the true and pure you. You started forgetting about the beautiful and powerful aspects of yourself and instead focused on the things that you thought you could control: your career, your purpose, and getting ahead. Isn't that what you were meant to do?

You found yourself doing things to prevent yourself from being with yourself and from feeling the impacts of the layer experiences. Choosing not to take time to reflect on what you were experiencing. Doing things to suppress the noise, feelings, and processing going on inside. You put others first, making them important and forgetting about yourself.

You read into other people's words and actions, and took them personally. At times, you found yourself putting up and shutting up, and felt responsible for other people and issues that were not yours. Smiling and laughing when inside you were crying. And giving and giving with little return. And others put you down and found fault in who you are and what you did, so you found fault in yourself too.

And within you, your emotions have been bubbling away, expressing themselves more dramatically when you react. Your mind has become like a Facebook post with lots of different responses. And you've been feeling the pull, the drain, and the impact of others' energy and the impact on you.

You react, your mind makes up stories or goes blank, you feel depressed at times, you doubt yourself, you don't feel good enough, and there are times you don't like who you are. However, you don't know how to change this. There are days where life feels hard, confusing, and even downright unfair. And you don't know who to talk to because the people you have raised things with don't understand. Also, no one really listened to you before, so why would it be any different now?

You are isolated emotionally and yet not physically. You are tired, feeling lots of things, and you are not sure what they are, where they come from, and why you are experiencing them. You just want to go to bed and hide, hide away from the world. However, what you are really doing is hiding away from yourself. So you just get busy. Busy with work, busy caring about others, busy doing something, anything, and busy running away from yourself.

How on earth do you know you need healing? How do you know whether what you are emotionally and physiologically feeling and what is going on in your head is normal or not? How do you know you are not coping? How do you know that what you keep experiencing is because of the impact of your conditioning? And how do you know you should talk about what is happening to you? How do you know what to talk about? How do you even describe it?

You don't know what to do about yourself … until a situation happens that floods you with vulnerability and emotion. That's what wakes you up to the need to heal. Finally, you get it. You see it, feel it, hear it in yourself, and you live it. That's when finally you know you need to do something.

You experience the internal crisis that ensues after an external experience triggers huge amounts of emotion. It hurts, it is out of control, it is depressing, it is devastating, you feel lost and lonely, you feel overwhelmed, and it feels like you claw your way back, ripping your nails apart, to some level of sanity. You experience things that shake your world apart, that shock you, that stop you in your stride and even knock you to the floor. You fall apart to rebuild.

So, do you wait for a crisis or an extreme event to shake you into action? If you do, then the action you take will be born out of desperation.

Or do you take the step to work proactively with your processing? So that when a crisis or situation that triggers emotional upheaval does happen, you are able to self-facilitate and manage your process through the experience, rather than it managing you? This is action derived from choice and personal power.

The I Make a Difference process shared in this book supports you to proactively work with your process. It supports you to know the answers to WHAT you are experiencing, WHY you are experiencing it, WHERE it comes from, and HOW to work with it. The I Make a Difference process provides the complete context, structure, and approach for identifying and working through your feelings, thoughts, and processing so that you build your resilience and learn how to identify what is happening within yourself and how to facilitate yourself through it.

Your Past and You

Your past—the layer experiences and their impacts—has a hold on you. And no matter how insignificant you believe some of your uncomfortable previous experiences were, especially if you are comparing them to other people's or to some of the more outstandingly painful ones you've had, these experiences impact you internally and influence your interactions externally.

The hold your past has on you is what is preventing you from connecting to and being the true you, the jewel within you. Past experiences, subconsciously and even consciously, infiltrate your thoughts, your dream time, your physiological state, and how you feel about and value yourself. Let alone your decision-making, your relationships, what you see, hear, how you interpret things, and how you live your life.

You are at the mercy of your past. Forgetting about it is only going to suppress it and make it more powerful in its influence on you. In "forgetting about it," what happens is that you bury it in your subconscious mind, so you are not even aware of it being there and the power it has over you. However, it is aware of and has control of you.

Like most of us, you were not taught to work with your emotions and the chatter in your head. Your inability to feel, deal with, and express your emotions in a healthy way has been going on for generations and generations. Your parents impacted you, their parents impacted them, and on it goes. You will impact your children.

However, you can change this. You can be free of the incessant mental, emotional, energy, physical, and depending on your beliefs, spiritual processing that stems from the impacts of your past.

You can heal the impacts of your past. You can dissolve the hold these experiences have on you, so you see the experiences you have had through different eyes. You will see them neutrally rather than as good, bad, negative or positive. And you'll see the benefit in everything you experience, knowing situations occur not to you, rather for you as a gift in your travels through life. Gifts to heal, discover, uncover, reclaim, reconnect, and connect to what is true for you, your life, and the true you. So you can allow yourself to not just shine, but glow. Glow with the light, radiance, joy, love, understanding, strength, and amazingness that you are.

What it requires is for you to open the door to your internal world and your processing. For you to shine a light on the areas within yourself that require your attention, so you can unravel your conditioning to heal and dissolve the impacts and layers from your past. In doing so, you uncover the light that is still within you. You begin to reclaim who you truly are as you reconnect to your jewel within, the jewel that is you.

This book is one of the gifts on your travels that will guide you on your inner adventure to discover the true you.

In These Pages

In opening this book, you are stepping into the I Make a Difference process to find your way through the multidimensional layers and aspects of yourself. The information and activities explored in this book provide you with in-depth and comprehensive guidance so that you can uncover the answers you have within yourself while having a structure that explains and supports you in understanding how you became who you are today and who you truly are. You'll find in the coming chapters numerous tools and approaches to apply in the exploration of yourself.

The foundation and essence of the I Make a Difference process is the I Make a Difference Onion Model, which you will begin to experience in chapter four. The Onion Model provides a detailed and structured picture of the pattern of how your process unfolds in the conditioning and impacts of your layer experiences. The Onion Model, in combination with the other approaches outlined in this book, provides guidance for exploring areas in yourself, so that you can look at, accept, explore, and work with these parts of yourself, in order to integrate all aspects of yourself and be whole again.

On your adventure of unravelling and healing your conditioning and connecting to your jewel within the following tools, approaches, and processes are what you will explore and experience on the pathway through this book:

- Free writing to download, process out, and let go what you are processing and experiencing
- Self-facilitation and the activities for exploring yourself
- Identifying and working with your mental, emotional, physical, energy, and spiritual processes
- The I Make a Difference Onion Model: understanding how you became who you are today, who you truly are, and working with your behaviors, emotions, and underlying issues to deeply connect with your jewel within
- The three phases of integration with yourself
- Your beliefs and identifying and growing your helpful ones; working with the limiting ones to know where they come from, releasing them, and creating new helpful beliefs
- Growing your ability to respond rather than react

- Working with the five steps of responding that assist with your understanding, acceptance, and development of yourself
- Identifying which stage of processing you are experiencing so that you can consciously work with your lessons, learning, uncovering, and discovering of your true and pure self

Yes, this book is for you, about you, and getting to truly know you.

You will also get to know about me on your adventure to rediscovering the true you as my life story is what facilitated the development of the I Make a Difference Onion Model as well as the tools, approaches, and processes explored within these pages. While you are introduced to my story in the next chapter, I will give you a brief overview here: I've spent most of my life studying myself and discovering the answers, tools, and processes within me, so I could discover and become the true me. I designed the I Make a Difference (IMAD) Personal Development Program in 2000.

For over fifteen years, in my IMAD programs, I have facilitated and walked beside thousands of individuals— from corporate business people to the traditional owners—the Aboriginal people of Australia to disengaged youth to incarcerated men and women. The aim for all of my program participants was the same as my aim for you in this book: to provide the map and tools for you to use to journey inside yourself and connect to your jewel within. Just as with the thousands of program participants, I want you to be resourced to be self-reliant in facilitating your inner adventure, so you can make a difference to yourself, your family, your community and for the generations to come.

The Differences Being Made

Why commit to healing, unravelling, rediscovering, and reconnecting to your jewel within? Because the differences that can be made are:

- People having the tools to be self-sufficient and self-empowered in facilitating their own healing, growth, and development.
- Individuals not taking their emotions and issues out on each other.
- Parents supporting their children to express their emotions in a healthy way and facilitating them to process out their experiences.
- Parents creating environments where children do not suppress, separate from, and lose who they truly are.
- People enjoying amazing relationships where they share their true selves and are open to receiving and experiencing what they truly deserve.
- Managers and leaders not being scared to facilitate their own and their employees' emotions in the workplace.
- People who are physically unwell having an aspect of their life where they have some power and influence over what is happening to them, i.e., their mental and emotional processing.
- People stopping the projection and imposition of their own issues and processes on each other.

- Children stopping having to parent adults.
- Children being allowed to be children.
- Adults becoming childlike and not childish.
- Adults stopping parenting adults.
- Adults learning to parent themselves.
- People stopping being scared to show emotion, so they can take responsibility and be who they truly are.
- People connecting to the jewel that is them.
- People giving themselves permission to be who they truly are.

Pause, Process, and Explore

A powerful way to explore yourself internally, grow your awareness and understanding of yourself so you can unravel your conditioning and work towards connecting to who you truly are is through exploring your processing in response to specific questions. There are many of these types of activities throughout the book. Chapter 3 provides a detailed introduction to these activities. In the meantime, I encourage you to get a notebook, journal, or a piece of paper and a pen or the IMAD Personal Processing Workbook you downloaded. (You can even choose to capture your answers in your phone or any other way that feels right for you.) Once you are ready, make some time to explore and discover the answers within yourself to the following questions:

a. What drew you to read this book?
b. What are the questions you have that you want to find answers to?

c. What areas in yourself do you want to learn about, explore, change, grow, and/or develop? And why?

d. What else would you like to achieve or gain from reading this book?

Trust the information that comes to you and capture your answers. The answers are what you think and feel and are right for you.

Through taking time now to respond to these questions, your responses will provide a valuable reference point for your growth and development. You can see where you are at now and where you move to. In the final chapter, you will refer back to these responses that you record now.

Note: I encourage you to write in a journal or elsewhere, rather than in this book. The reason being, you could come back to the book in a month, six months, or a couple of years to go back over the information and the activities. You will have grown, developed, and evolved, and what you have previously written in the book could influence your processing.

Your Commitment to Yourself

This is not the start of your process. This is the continuation and extension of everything you have done to this point. I Make a Difference is an opportunity to reinforce what you know is true and right for you. To uncover and discover more of what is true for you and the true you. And for you to put into action doing right by you.

There is no quick fix to healing and developing yourself. It takes time. And it takes your willingness. It takes your belief that it is possible. And it takes the want to grow your awareness of your internal processing. As well as your ability to see every change that you make and experience, from the minuscule through to the significant. It takes your ability to ask for help. And it takes your acceptance that this is a process that takes time and the length of time it takes is unique to you and influenced by how open you are to yourself.

If you identify that you require support or have a question or story you would like to share, I welcome you to contact me: *melinda@imakeadifferenceimad.com* and *www.imakeadifferenceimad.com*. If you find that you would like some regular personal processing sessions with me, that's an option we can discuss together. Don't hesitate to reach out. I am available.

To truly live the I Make a Difference adventure I encourage and ask you to experience this book as you read it. Feel it. Feel the mental, emotional, physiological, energy, physical and spiritual processing. Experience your process and work with your processing. Embody everything you are reading, make friends with all aspects of yourself, and get to know what each part of you feels like, looks like, sounds like, and how each part operates and unfolds. This is the way you will make a true difference with and to you.

If you find yourself searching for answers outside of yourself, you will explore and change less of what is going on inside of yourself. This process is about you going inwards, into you, and finding for yourself the answers that lie within.

As already mentioned, the first stop on your adventure inside yourself is learning the origins of the I Make a Difference process and program, so that means learning a bit about me. That's what you will explore in chapter 2.

CHAPTER 2

HOW I BECAME IMAD

You know those times when you feel really alone in the world, and what you are doing feels like same old, same old? You feel numb, then empty, and powerless. You hope and even pray for that miracle to happen to save you and make you and your life better. Umm ... and you wait and wait. *I lived in that space, not just for months, it was for years until I realized if I wanted to make a difference to what was happening in my life, I would have to make a difference to how I felt inside myself.*

As this book's I Make a Difference process was born out of my own journey and is intrinsically intertwined with my story, this is what we will explore in this chapter: my adventures and the origins of the I Make a Difference process. Come travel with me.

Start of the Separation

It it had not been for the reference point of unconditional love from my grandfather and the support from my mother, when she could, I would not have reached the point in my life to write this book.

I spent the first five years of my life cocooned in a bubble of unconditional love from my grandfather (my father was adopted, so my grandfather was not my biological grandparent). Little did I know that behind the scenes, there were undertones of rejection being projected at me, which I found out many years later.

Unbeknown to me: my non-biological grandmother, Grandma, informed my maternal biological Nana that she (Nana) could have me because she (Grandma) wanted my brother. And my father had already threatened to leave my mother when she'd shared she was pregnant with me.

These interactions and the energy attached to them influenced the start of the change of me—my separation from my true self.

I remember the first time I was beaten (as opposed to being hit). I was nine years old. It was for something I knew inside myself I was not to do, so I didn't do it. However, this was not aligned with what others (adults) wanted me to do.

The beating is the first clear recollection I have where I felt within me, a separation take place from who I was, to who I became in that moment. The feeling of a hard coldness embodying me and a fierce independence that kicked in. I knew that I was on my own, the world was unsafe, and I had to fight my battles myself. And the realization that I was not believed, there was no one there to protect and support me, and I was alone. I was punished for trusting myself and what I knew was right.

I was raised in a dysfunctional, distorted, alcohol-fueled, and abusive environment. I learned to become aggressive, competitive, and tough. I didn't fit anywhere,

I felt rejection easily, I reacted sensationally, and I was filled with self-loathing. I can now see that from a young age, I started putting up personas, creating layers, and separating from who I truly was— all elements of our conditioning that we will explore later in the book.

Over the years, I experienced my parents' fights and anger. At eleven I saw my father being physically abusive with my mother. So, I broke his arm with my hockey stick. From that day on I became my mother's protector. Protecting her from physical pain and redirecting the fights towards me.

This was the creation of a pattern that impacted my life for years to come: I became the rescuer and protector of many people, fighting fights that were not mine, when actually I was the one who wanted to be rescued. I remember the screaming inside of me, "Would someone please just stick up for me for once?!"

My male friends didn't protect me as they said they didn't need to. I did such a good job of sticking up for myself. I had filled the space, leaving no room for anyone else to step in and defend me.

My neediness for people to like me for who I was, not how I looked, grew out of the energy I had felt off some older men in my life where I felt uncomfortable. I learned to downplay my looks, adopt a tomboy approach, not wear makeup, wear simple clothing, and be outspoken (a great defensive technique). Another persona, more suppression, and another layer. And this only contributed to fueling my feelings of jealousy toward "feminine" females where I felt I was not good enough. What I was doing? Rejecting my own femininity.

During my teens, my friends used to call me "tough chick should have been a brick." I used to laugh and think that was cool. This was me covering up what was really going on inside me.

There were only one or two people who had an inkling of what was going on in my family and how I was truly feeling. The dynamics of my home environment had conditioned me to be staunch, aggressive, and strong. Anger was how I expressed myself, and yet underneath the hurt was tearing me apart inside.

Little did I know until many years later that a number of the girls at school were scared of me. The sadness I felt when I heard this. What had I been showing people? The sadness was for me and what I had I done to myself. Who had I become?

I remember when I was 18, sitting on my bed and promising myself that I would not have children until I had healed myself. Where I was no longer a product of my conditioning or upbringing.

I ran away. I travelled for a number of years in my late teens and early twenties. I was running away from home, my emotional turmoil, and myself. Yet everywhere I went the emotional turbulence came with me.

When I turned 21, I started to unravel, physically, emotionally, mentally, and energy-wise. Experience after experience kept occurring, including having my front tooth knocked out on my 21st birthday. And each experience resulted in me becoming more and more out of control internally. I became desperate to find ways to control and suppress my mind chatter, paranoia, and emotions.

My initial solution: smoke lots of pot. This will numb me. It certainly does when you smoke it all your waking hours. Then friends kicked my butt, telling me, "Sort your shit out," and I stopped.

I became anorexic and bulimic. I didn't eat, and if on the odd occasion I did have a morsel, I threw it up. I believed I had to be skinny to be loved in a relationship. I believed I was not good enough in any way to be loved. My focus was on how I looked, not who I was. Anorexia and bulimia offered me a way to keep my emotional turmoil at bay. The sad part was how much I was rejecting every aspect of myself.

The Beginning of the Change to Find Me

Upon returning from overseas, I was a wreck emotionally, mentally, and physically. Mum hated seeing me this way and did everything she could to help me. She exposed me to meditation, astrology, philosophy, and to Shirley MacLaine's series of books. I gobbled these up in my desperate search to find some semblance of peace within myself. And it helped to a point.

I had to do something, I was so absorbed in my own misery, self-pity, and shit. I wanted something to crack me, to explode me and help me come out of my misery and learn about compassion. My knowing kept screaming, "Go to India!" so I did.

I related India to being a country of compassion, and I wanted to find this in me. What I did discover is how judgmental I was. I had made an assumption that the people I saw who lived on the streets in India were worse off than me. The reality is that they were so much happier than I had ever been.

India was confronting on so many levels, and yet every part of my being craved the simplicity of just being me. I recall a taxi driver harassing me for more money. The tough Melinda was nowhere to be found, and at that moment I burst into tears. This was not me, I didn't cry, and yet I could not stop the crying. The cracks were happening. The care and support I received from this man in response to my tears showed me that being real and vulnerable was safe.

I journeyed to the Bihar School of Yoga, where I stayed for a time. No, not to learn yoga (always struggled with doing that one). My mother had exposed me to ashrams, as it was an interest and a savior for her. I was a non-conformist, so I knew I would not stay, but I knew there was something I was to find while I was there.

I chose to be initiated. For me, this process was about me making a commitment to myself to find out who I truly was. I was given the Sanskrit name Manikootananda. And I was told this means "jewel at the top of the mountain." Swami Satyananda, the head of the ashram at the time, gave me this name because of what he saw in me, which at that time I could not see. Other resident swamis asked me what was the name Swami Satyananda had given me. In response they told me that I would be a guiding light to others for them to find the jewel within themselves.

I struggled to accept this, as my self-worth was so lacking and there was no way I deserved to be able to do this. What I did know is I wanted to be that jewel for myself. Little did I know what was to come.

Around the age of 25, the control tactics I had applied on myself, the anorexia and bulimia, and then obsessive sport, that had been suppressing my emotions, finally crumbled. I not only exploded but imploded, and I fell apart. I fell into the emotions I had suppressed and had been running away from for years.

A situation of extreme proportions happened, which triggered the collapse of the control. I received a letter in which I was threatened with having my knees blown out and other actions taken against me and my brother. I was petrified. All the venom, violence, rejection, anger, hurt, extreme fear, and dysfunctional crap from my childhood and life began to surface.

In amongst the internal haze, darkness, and insanity I was going through, I became aware that I knew I had something very unique, special, and precious inside me. Something which if I could not see it, feel it, or touch it, how could anyone else? I knew I now needed to truly take the step to make a difference to how I felt inside of myself.

I needed help.

And the option was a formal process with a therapist to assist me in my journey of facing myself, healing myself, and reclaiming who I truly was and am. At the time I wasn't fully aware this was what I was doing. I was just trying to get through a day without being paralyzed by fear and hiding in a room or worse.

The conventional therapist process was brilliant in creating the space without judgement for me to express what was happening to me. Finally, a safe space for me with someone who got most of it and would listen to me. I felt better during the period of these sessions; however, it was when I got home that the turmoil of my emotions, the insane self-talk and paranoia in my head, returned.

The tools the therapist offered didn't work for me. They were theoretical and conceptual, and I could not grasp what I was to do.

The Answers Within Me

I wanted to heal what I was feeling, not just have temporary relief. I knew I had the answers inside of myself, and I wanted to find the pathway inwards to discover them. I needed to find my own internal practical, tangible processes that I could use to help myself unravel my conditioning, work with the impacts of my past, heal myself, and not be reliant on others for this to happen.

Being fiercely independent, as I had been let down a lot by others, I chose to study myself internally. I explored my processing, my emotions and began to discover ways that helped me to start healing the impacts of my past. And I was determined to discover Melinda, the real me.

I started developing my way of facilitating myself in working with my conditioning and processing in my search to find and feel my connection to that precious jewel within myself. The beautiful me I remembered and knew that I was when I was with my grandfather in his unconditional love and acceptance. I had to create the same space my grandfather shared with me. I committed totally to my journey of personal growth and development, and it became a fascination for me. My purpose in life became to find and be me.

There were many days, weeks, months, and years I spent alone and lonely. Relationship breakups. Being an adult student while my peers were getting married, having children, and establishing their careers. Living hand to mouth, and living with the turmoil within myself.

The pain, the roller coaster, the days, weeks, and months of crying, desperation, and the feeling of unworthiness. Then the moments of hope in feeling an hour of quiet space internally. Question after question after question. And the explosions, venom, and hatred I felt. The depression and not wanting to be here. And the believing that the grieving and pain within would never change. There were many times I wanted to give up, but I knew in my knowing deep down inside of myself that one day it would be different. And it was.

I began finding the answers I needed for myself within myself. And I was discovering and developing tools and approaches that enabled me to work with the process of unravelling and healing myself. I was living and creating my process of development, rather than reading about it or being told about it.

I still couldn't shake the feeling of not being loved. Then a woman asked me, "Do you believe you were born lovable?"

My immediate answer: "No. That's obvious by how I have been treated and rejected."

She asked me again, "Do you believe you were born lovable?"

Once I got over my initial defensive reaction, it dawned on me that I wasn't born a reject. I was born that beautiful person I remembered and knew I was. It was other people's inability to show their love that was projected onto me, which left me feeling unlovable. Every child is born lovable. So my own healing was happening, and I was also discovering who I truly was.

This realization and process supported me to start seeing how a number of the painful experiences in my life were not my fault. They were not my issue and most importantly not my responsibility. These experiences impacted me and I had taken them on and made them mine—when they weren't all mine.

Changes were happening internally, and I felt them. Initially, this was all that was important to me as no matter what happened externally if I did not feel different internally, then what was the point? I also knew that change on the outside would come as a result of how I was on the inside.

My Work, an Expression of My Personal Process

Professionally I journeyed into the world of training. This involved facilitating corporate training with big organizations, involving managers, employees, and supervisors. The training programs I delivered included communication skills, team building, and leadership.

During my delivery of these training programs, I discovered that when I put the content to the side and explored the real issues the participants had and asked the appropriate questions, the participants already had the answers and solutions for what they needed to do.

Over time I became dissatisfied with traditional corporate training methods, which involved the rehashing of the same processes, ideas, and concepts. I knew real change came from people owning the process themselves. I knew people had the answers inside of themselves as to what was right for their work environment, families, and themselves. The key was for me, as the facilitator, to walk beside them and be invisible in their process so that they owned it as I facilitated it.

As I had been facilitating my own process for changing myself internally, I grew my ability to facilitate others in developing their ability to work with their own processes themselves—where they find the answers that they already have within themselves and are empowered to take responsibility for Identifying and implementing the actions they know are right for them.

I met a like-minded trainer, Dougal, at this time, and we created a business together. We worked together on developing our own unique way of facilitating. Our approach was to create an environment where we facilitated people to uncover and discover the answers within themselves, to voice those answers, and to commit to putting them into action. Ownership and responsibility of the actions and outcomes came from people having input.

Dougal and I worked with a number of businesses in facilitating the development of their culture, teams, and the leadership of the managers.

As we were Melinda and Dougal we called ourselves MaD. Initially, I suggested that it stood for "Movement and Discovery." However, it was our wise logo designer who changed it to "Make a Difference," a name far more reflective of the work we were doing.

Creating IMAD

In 2000, when our MaD work became quiet, in my needy state I remember asking people close to me, "What am I meant to be doing? What is my purpose?" They reflected back the Sanskrit name I had been given—Manikootananda—and what it meant: jewel at the top of the mountain. I had forgotten all about it. I had been working on discovering the jewel within myself, the true me. Now it was time to put my personal process into something others could access and connect to.

At the same time, Mere, my best friend, became a work colleague. This happened not long after Dougal chose to leave our business. His comment to me was, "You are the heart-and-soul person, and I am the logic person."

Work had been slim on the ground, and after Dougal left, it dried up. After I shared what was happening work-wise, an astrologer I respected encouraged me to do something creative. That's when it came to me: I would utilize this time to design the personal development program I had always wanted to create.

The words from my knowing and truth were, "Now is the time to create what you are to do," and the reinforcement was in the messages from the environment. I surrendered my efforts in trying to create work. I knew that if I had to put so much effort into things where the energy was not being reciprocated, then there was something else for me to do and focus on.

I got some temping work to pay the bills and began the eight-month process of designing the program. This was the coming together of the most important processes in my life that I had been working with: self-facilitation, facilitation of others, development of training programs, the love of human processes and processing, combined with personal growth and development.

As Make a Difference was the business name, the obvious and totally appropriate name for the program readily came to me: "I Make a Difference."

I was committed to designing a program that would facilitate individuals to develop their awareness and understanding of themselves, meaning their internal and external processing, and that would provide them with the tools to self-facilitate their own internal healing process to reclaim who they were born as and are. It was a program that would support independence rather than co-dependence. And a program for people to discover the jewel that lies within themselves.

My journey was focused on me discovering, creating, and applying tools and approaches that were real, practical, and tangible. What I would share with others I had experienced myself, so I knew what was possible in the healing of yourself and the reclaiming of who you truly are.

My eight months designing the I Make a Difference program involved me becoming conscious of and identifying every emotion, every thought, and every behavior, as well as every sensation, every feeling, and every process I had experienced. There was a pattern to all of it, and I was going to discover it.

I ran with the natural process of designing this program and the process unfolded. It had a significant pattern to it that came together like magic. This was the first time I was conscious of trusting the process. My fascination, my curiosity, and my love of human process and processing grew and grew.

Out of all of this, I created the I Make a Difference Onion Model, the foundational structure of the I Make a Difference, IMAD, program and process. The Onion Model, which chapters 4 to 7 are dedicated to, describes how we become who we are today and who we truly are.

The I Make a Difference program provided individuals with a period of time to totally focus on themselves and their processing while experiencing an internal experiential process—one where they could grow their awareness of their processing internally, their awareness of what they were feeling, thinking, sensing, knowing, and why they were experiencing it. Where they grew their awareness of their behaviors, the impacts they had on others, and the impacts others had on them. Most importantly the program was for individuals to find the source of where all the impacting processing—the emotional turmoil, the mental anguish, the physiological sensations of anxiety and other uncomfortable physical sensations they experienced—came from, and for them to be resourced with choices as to the tools and approaches they could apply to unravel and heal those impacts.

Delivering IMAD

IMAD and University Students—in 2001 the first 3.5-day I Make a Difference Personal Leadership and Development Program was delivered (later I developed it into a 5- to 7-day program). Soon after, two more followed involving groups of Auckland University students who belonged to AIESEC, an international youth-led organization.

These initial IMAD participants were from a range of cultural backgrounds, studying all types of degrees. The processing they did back then and where they have now grown to is amazing in the dimensions of the lives they lead, the work they do, and the relationships they have.

That same year public IMAD programs began. When I say "public" IMAD programs, these are programs for any individual over the age of 15 from the general public who either heard or read about the program and registered to attend. The people who attended were from a broad range of cultural and religious backgrounds, their ages varied from 16 through to 73. They were single, married, divorced, and from a variety of different work environments.

IMAD and Incarcerated Men and Women—the New Zealand Department of Corrections contracted Make a Difference to deliver the I Make a Difference program to both female and male inmates, separately. Our role was not to judge the individuals for what they had done, but rather to assist them as people to heal, grow, and develop. Mere and I were conscious of checking—*do we have any judgements? Are we being neutral with the participants? What reactions have we had and why?* This was an opportunity for Mere and me to check in on our growth and development.

A number of inmates discovered the original layer situation that led them to be in prison. They found their "why" and gained a greater depth of understanding as to their choices and what they had done. Next, the healing. Each person had a history, a story, and experiences that had been impacting on them. We did not condone what they had done; however, we could understand how they had reached the point they had. With IMAD they now had different options and choices as to how they could make a difference in their own lives.

IMAD and Business People—we soon had the opportunity to deliver the I Make a Difference program to individuals in the business world. Employees, leading hands, supervisors, managers, and members of human resources attended. Their intention was to develop their ability to self-facilitate their own processing and understanding of themselves and other people. In turn, this would support them to grow their ability to lead more effectively and to facilitate fellow employees and situations.

Though the ultimate aim was to increase their abilities to facilitate individuals, meetings, teams, and training sessions in the business world, the focus of the IMAD program was on each participant personally. The feedback they shared both during and afterwards was that they experienced significant valuable changes in their home lives, and the enhancement of their relationships with their spouses and children had a beneficial flow-on effect to their workplace. Admittedly, this feedback warmed my soul.

IMAD and Australia

In 2006 my knowing was strong in the message that I had to move to Australia. So I moved myself, my cat, and my business to Aussie. However, there already was a business called Make a Difference in Australia, so I changed the name of my business to Globally Make a Difference (GMAD).

In Australia, the South Australia government with the support of local business contracted GMAD to be a part of one of the biggest ever pre-employment programs. It was a 20-week program with one hundred participants, and my business was responsible for the leadership and personal development of the participants. Can you imagine what it was like doing eight IMADs, of five days in duration each, over twenty weeks—as well as the other key programs that we designed and delivered that went with it? It was a lot of responsibility and energy—and an incredible opportunity for us at GMAD and the participants alike!

The participants included long-term unemployed traditional owners—the Aboriginal people of Australia. And disengaged youth, individuals with ankle bracelets, and ex-inmates. As well as individuals who had experienced workplace injuries and people who had never worked a day in their lives.

The local businesses of South Australia knew they could provide the skills training to these individuals. The key area the businesses didn't have the capability to support was in regard to these individuals' self-confidence, self-belief, self-worth, emotional processing, and conditioned behaviors. This is why I Make a Difference became a critical element to the success of these individuals and to other work readiness programs we were involved with. Eighty-seven of the one hundred participants graduated and gained employment.

IMAD and Disengaged Youth—next Globally Make a Difference worked in partnership with TAFE and industry to develop and deliver a work readiness program purely for disengaged youth. These young people had been told by people from all areas of their life that they were useless, they wouldn't amount to anything, and they would never get a job. They had dropped out of school, they couldn't get employment, some were in foster care, and their behaviors were sometimes off the Richter scale.

They were awesome. Their ages were from sixteen to twenty-one. There were two girls and twenty-something boys. Their growth in confidence, ability, awareness, and maturity was exceptional. A number of them gained apprenticeships and employment with companies.

I am still aware of the progress of the two girls, Shakenna and Zoe. They became fully qualified trades women working for some of the biggest mining companies in Australia. If only you had met them when they started the course. Shakenna appeared to be shy and did not say much, except to pull the guys into line. Zoe would swear her head off and was a tough chick (umm, sounds like someone I knew well!). To see where they are at now is amazing. The essence of who they are is the same; however, they shine in their belief in themselves and the valuing of who they are. We knew they could do it; they just needed to know it.

Young people, and actually all of us, just want to be understood and accepted. Then we feel safe enough to be who we really are and drop our protection. Sometimes we just need someone else to believe in us in order to find belief in ourselves.

I'll add too because of my neediness to be of value (you will explore neediness in the IMAD Onion Model chapter 7) and also because it is evidence of the impacts of IMAD—even the local magistrate emailed saying that the

I Make a Difference program had contributed to the reduction in crime in the region. Wow.

IMAD and the Traditional Owners—the Aboriginal People of Australia—during the time of the first work readiness program, we met the mother of one of the Aboriginal men on the program. She was an elder in her community. She commented, "You are going to work with so many of our people." Little did I know what was to come and how right she was.

From 2008 to 2014 I, along with new facilitators that I employed, delivered the I Make a Difference program as an important part of the work readiness programs we were involved with. From 2010 onwards, the programs were solely for the traditional owners—the Aboriginal people of Australia, supporting their employment in the construction, retail, and mining industries. We delivered programs across South Australia, Northern Territory, Western Australia, and Mildura (Victoria). From 2013 onwards, other groups of individuals participated in our programs, including disengaged youth, individuals with disabilities, migrants, and refugees.

Yet again I learned so much about process and processing from walking alongside the Aboriginal people of Australia. I so so miss them. Their truth, their purity, their sensory process, and their ability to say it as it is. Their embracing of you once they know you are real. The simplicity of just being with them, the sharing of their culture, the beauty of the world through their eyes. And their comments like, "You swear too much, Melinda," or to my mother, "You talk too much." Thank you, Delvina and Vanessa, for saying it as it is. We will never forget you.

IMAD and Migrants and Refugees—then the migrants and refugees I met. They opened up a whole new world to me. Hearing their stories of what they escaped from in their homelands and the incredible and unbelievable journeys that led them to Australia. They allowed me to gain insight into their cultures, beliefs, and sense of community. Also their religion, hardships, passions, survival, appreciation, and who they are as individuals.

I had the honor to walk beside many individuals in providing training and processes that enabled them to rediscover their belief in themselves. Where they built their confidence and knew they deserved more from life. They gained qualifications, and for many of them, this was the first time they had completed something in their life. As importantly, my GMAD and also my Culturally Make a Difference (CMAD) employees and I worked with many large organizations where these individuals were able to gain employment, and the organizations went through a change in their culture.

My Business, More Personal Growth

In 2008 I became an employer. I consciously worked with the I Make a Difference program as the foundation of the culture of my business. I was committed to employees having time for their processing and being supported in their personal development and growth. Attendance on the I Make a Difference program was part of the recruitment process.

My journey as an employer. Wow, that is another whole long, long story, with some bizarre, crazy, and sad experiences, which now make me smile.

My professional experience became a critical part of my healing of myself and reclaiming of who I really am. From 2008 to 2016 as an employer of people and as an owner of businesses, what I experienced in eight years most people would not even experience in their lifetime. Every tiny bit of vulnerability I still had within myself for healing, something happened externally to ensure it was triggered, that it surfaced, and that I worked with it. I spent many days, weeks, and even a year or so crying in my business because of what I was experiencing. There were days I was actually scared to enter my own organization, which is really sad.

Some of the experiences could have made me harder, bitter, and cynical, or just give up. I didn't, I stayed with every process, knowing it was happening for a reason. The key reason first and foremost was for my personal healing, growth, and development, and that this would be expressed in the I Make a Difference program.

In 2016 I had to face the reality that it was time to put my businesses into liquidation. I had been saying for a while that by the end of 2016 I wanted to have sold the businesses, employed someone to run them, or some other option. This was so I could write my books and get back to the I Make a Difference process.

I knew.

I had held onto the businesses believing it was all I had and that I would be a failure if I had to close them. What would I do? And I didn't want to let down the amazing people who had walked beside me, not just as my employees but my friends.

You can't fight what is meant to be, what your path is.

As my mother put it, my time of volunteering was over. I felt a failure financially. I knew what I was doing was right. Yillie, my friend, said to me, "You may not have been a financial success, but you have been a huge success in the changes you have facilitated for so many people, which will continue on in their families for generations."

She was right, why I kept going was because of the people. My love of them, my love of what we did, the spaces we created where individuals were empowered to make a real difference in their lives.

The people we worked with gained so much, and it was so powerful and amazing, during these years. I also learned so much. And I grew and benefited enormously from an uncomfortable, painful, hurtful, glorious and treasured time. Every area I held vulnerability around was in my face.

Years earlier at the ashram in India, Swami Satyananda told me, "Whilst you have youth on your side, go and experience everything you can and lose your dependency on everyone and everything."

I pictured travelling the world and those types of experiences. Little did I know that the experiences I was to have involved facing the situations that allowed me to feel every impact of my past that I had suppressed so I could work with healing myself emotionally, mentally, energy-wise, physically and spiritually.

And losing my dependence on everyone and everything, my journey was one of finding the answers inside me, rather than books and other people.

I remember a colleague saying to me he was amazed at the amount I had been through professionally let alone personally. All these experiences not only helped me heal; they were also opportunities for me to relate to others and examples to share for each of the areas of the I Make a Difference process. All of it made sense.

Coming Home

I returned to New Zealand in 2016 with my partner, Alan, who has been such a huge part of my journey in more ways than I could have ever imagined. And also my cats.

I was returning home to the country where I was born, which was symbolic of the cycle of the journey I had been through to come home to myself. In returning home, I have had the space to reflect on what a long way I have travelled from where I was. I am so more the real me than I have ever been. My life is now about shining my jewel, exploring my own amazing qualities and attributes, expressing who I am and making a difference in my world outside of myself. I still discover new aspects of myself each day, less of the unravelling and healing and more of the uncovering and discovering—elements you will find out more about later in the book.

When I created the I Make a Difference program, I wanted to provide a process that would support people to become self-reliant in being able to facilitate their own healing and dissolving of the conditioned and hurtful impacts of their past, so they could discover the jewel within themselves. And this is what I have been doing. Through your reading this book and exploring the I Make a Difference process in the following chapters, you are not only on your journey, you are now part of my journey and I am a part of yours.

Before you journey farther into the I Make a Difference adventure, I want to ensure you have the necessary travel essentials. The following chapter provides you with this necessary information and guidance for immersing yourself in the I Make a Difference process.

PREPARATION FOR YOUR ADVENTURE INSIDE: THE I MAKE A DIFFERENCE ONION MODEL

As your I Make a Difference adventure involves exploring the elements, aspects, depths, and dimensions of yourself, it is important that you are prepared for this deep, extensive dive. Like the process airplane attendants guide us through before take-offs, I want to ensure that you have the background information, understanding of terminology, and a few other essential items to support you on your adventure. That's what this chapter supplies.

CORE BELIEFS

When you travel to different places, you may prepare yourself with exploring what the culture is like, the people, and the history. This assists in you making the most of your adventure. Similarly, it is important for you to gain some understanding of the beliefs and processing that underpin the I Make a Difference process.

During your travels, you don't absorb or agree with everything the people do, and you embrace the things that feel right for you. It is the same as your adventure through the I Make a Difference process. You'll encounter beliefs, ideas, and ways that you love and embrace, and possibly others that you don't. That's part of the journey.

The following are the core beliefs that support the I Make a Difference process. Be aware of particular beliefs that align with yours, and if there are beliefs that you don't connect with, they provide an opportunity for you to identify what it is that you do believe.

Core Belief**—**your past does not make you who you are. These experiences provide you with insight into all the different aspects of yourself, what is right for you and not right for you, and what you are actually capable of.

Your past and the layer experiences impact and condition you. However, they do not make you who you are; who you truly are is who you were born as.

If you were born into the ideal world where you were supported to be who you truly are and where others accepted your emotions, you would not need to be searching for the true you. You would be you.

Core Belief**—**you have a jewel at the core of who you are. You deserve to see it, feel it, and own your jewel.

Every person I have met has a jewel at the core of who they are. The goodness, beauty, purity, love, and other amazing qualities and attributes that are within their jewel are who they truly are. This is true for you as well. I have not met anyone whose core is different.

Core Belief**—**you, like every person, have the answers inside yourself. The answers you need for your growth, development, and life. And inside you also resides truth—you know what is right and wrong and what is right and wrong for you.

You have all the answers you ever need for yourself and your life within you. Where? Within what I term "your knowing." This is the place of purity inside you, which is untouched by the outside world. It is where your jewel and your truth reside.

You may call it your "gut feeling." And if you focus internally and feel the difference between the terms "gut feeling" and "knowing," then "gut feeling" is where you do not fully own what you know. When you own it as "your knowing," you take full ownership of what you know.

You already know what the right and wrong things are to do. You know what is truly right for you. The more you live from your knowing and your truth, the more you act on the right thing, the right thing for you and by you.

Core Belief—the process for healing your mental and emotional processing from the past is through parenting yourself.

When you are dependent on others for your emotional well-being, happiness, and emotional safety and security, you make them your parent. You make them responsible for how you feel. No other adult is responsible for another adult's emotional well-being. No child is responsible for an adult's emotional well-being.

The only person who can heal you is you.

Any emotional and mental processing you experience from your layer experiences is a part of you that is operating at the age you were when the layer experience happened. So when you parent yourself, who you are parenting is the child within you at the age you were when that experience occurred. In this way, you are responsible for your own emotional well-being.

***Core Belief*—the only thing that is negative in life is a negative charge. All emotions are exactly that—emotions.**

When you classify emotions, experiences, behaviors, and any other thing, as "negative" or "positive," you are making a judgement. You are making something right or wrong based on your experience, beliefs, and emotions. This will impact your receptiveness to what you are judging. Especially your receptiveness to healing your emotions.

Emotions and experiences are just that—they are emotions and experiences. So, state the facts.

Your emotions and experiences will have had an impact on you, and this is what you describe. The impact may have been one of joy and happiness, or discomfort, pain, and being overwhelmed.

When you cease personalizing emotions and experiences, you are able to see them for what they are rather than your judgement of them. You accept them more readily, which enables you to work with them without, or with less, resistance.

***Core Belief*—language and communication have significant impacts on people's emotional, mental, physical, and energy processing, including your own. Be**

conscious of the language you use and state what you truly mean.

We are not as conscious about what we say as we can be. The words we use have significant impacts on our processing. The definition of a word can be different from the conditioning and mental, emotional, and physical impacts of that word on an individual's processing. For example, take the word "challenge." Individuals I have worked with have explored internally the feeling and processing attached to the word "challenge" and what it means to them. It has been described as "up for a fight," "competition," "I have to prove myself," "a risk I have to take," "I am going to be challenged," and "I am scared."

In turn, the impact for some people when they hear the word "challenge" is that they rev themselves up to take on the challenge, others want to fight, some want to win, some get scared, and some shy away from it.

Because words invoke many different internal reactions, different interpretations, and processing, be specific and bring the situation back to basics and use words that describe it for what it is rather than your judgement of it.

For example, you could view a "challenge" as an "opportunity for growth." This is an emotionally neutral phrase that supports receptivity to the activity.

Core Belief—everything you experience happens for a reason and for your benefit. It is how you view it and what you look for that influences this.

It is often not till some time after an event, a minute, an hour, a day, a week, a month or many years later, that we discover the reason for what we experienced. Then we say, "Hindsight is a wonderful thing."

When you want to know the answer straight away, your vulnerability and emotional neediness are driving this because you want to feel emotionally safe and secure. So you go looking for some miracle in the process, some big reason for the pain, hardship, and discomfort you are going through.

You are also likely to view experiences as either good or bad. You do this because of how you are feeling about the experience, rather than viewing the experience as an experience (see previous core belief) and identifying the gifts you can gain from it.

There is a beautiful reason for each step of each process that you go through. Look at what is happening now and focus on this moment in time. See the gifts, learnings, discoveries, and value you gain from the experience. Look at how you can benefit from what is happening, what the gift is for you.

***Core Belief*—you can handle whatever happens to you in life because you have done so up until now.**

If you are reading this, then you have handled everything you have experienced in life up till now. What you experienced may have been horrible, painful, uncomfortable, or joyful. You have handled getting through all of those times.

With greater awareness and with unravelling the conditioning of your past and healing your emotions, you will handle what happens in your life more powerfully.

***Core Belief*—there are no failures or mistakes (unless stated by law). These are opportunities for growth and development.**

Viewing an experience, action, word, feeling, outcome, or situation as a failure or mistake is you judging you. It means you have an emotional attachment to what you have judged about yourself and you are rejecting it—and yourself.

Everything you experience is an opportunity for growth and development. Release the judgements and rejection, embrace the experience and your part in it, and gain the most from it.

These core beliefs provide important background information and insight into the culture of the I Make a Difference process. Another crucial aspect to IMAD is the focus on "process" and "processing" as they are essential to your experience.

PROCESS AND PROCESSING

Your coming adventure with the I Make a Difference process involves two significant experiences to be aware of to embrace and immerse yourself in. They have been mentioned a few times: process and processing. Having an understanding of what they involve will support you in being familiar with navigating them.

Process

Why on earth is the process so prominent in this book and the I Make a Difference program? Why is it important?

Process is the natural way something operates, works, and unfolds. A process can be set or random, fluid, transforming, and constantly moving. When a process is blocked, it is because something is stopping and controlling it.

On the I Make a Difference adventure, consider the process a journey from one point to another, to an outcome, conclusion, realization, or pausing point. Then this same process transforms into a new one and moves to a different place. It is the steps and flow of something. In being aware of each of the processes involved in the healing and developing of yourself, you are more aware of what potentially will unfold, which will support you to be more effective in facilitating yourself through the unfolding.

A key process you will experience is the I Make a Difference Onion Model process. This is the process of how you separated from your true self as a child to become who you are today, and all the elements to work with and unravel to return to the true you. As you explore yourself and the Onion Model process, you have both internal and external processes to focus and shine your light on.

Your Internal Processes

Mental process—the process you experience in your mind that involves memories, thoughts, words, conversations, stories, pictures, and beliefs.

Emotional process—the process that involves emotions you feel, physiological sensations, such as butterflies, a lump in the throat, the holding your breath, and knots in the stomach. As well as temperature and energy changes.

Sensory process—the process of energy changes, vibrations, hearing, taste, smell, touch. As well as the energy, emotions, and intentions you pick up off others; what you sense.

Physical process—the process you experience in your physical body: tightening, aches, headaches, physical release, and muscle memory.

Energy process—the process that is separate from your physical energy; this is your life force, the energy that flows through you, which is impacted by all of the other processes. You can experience feeling drained, backstabbed, tired, light, energized, heavy, or blocked.

Spiritual process—the process that is influenced by and defined by what spirituality means to you.

Qualities and attributes process—the process that is about the essence of who you are. What qualities and attributes lie at the core of you and how they influence your decision-making, communication, interactions, and expression.

Knowing process—this is where the purity of who you are lies. This is your jewel, your soul, and your truth. This is where all the answers you need for yourself reside.

Your internal processes influence and impact your external processes, so external processes require your attention too.

Your External Processes

Behavior process—what you do, the actions you take, the expressions on your face, your hand movements, and your stance.

Speech process—the words and tone you use, the pitch of your voice, the volume and the speed or your speech.

Hearing process —what you choose to hear and not hear. Whether you listen to yourself or others.

Sight process—what you choose to see and not see. Whether your focus is on yourself or others.

Smell process—what you choose to smell and not smell.

Touch process—what you choose to touch and not touch.

Your impact process—what you, directly and indirectly, do to others.

Then there are other external processes that require your consideration and awareness that can impact your internal processes and then your external processes.

Other people's external processes—their behavior, words, energy, looks, intentions, and emotions and how they influence and impact you.

Other people's internal processes—what others emit in their energy, intentions, and emotions and its impact on you.

The nature of the relationships you have with others has a process to them, whether they are familiar, informal, professional, the level of emotional attachment, and even roles and responsibilities influence your interactions and processing in this type of process.

The environment you are in has a process that impacts you. The physical environment, sound, lighting, heat, comfort, air circulation, and size are some of the key elements that have an influence on you.

In response to reading about these processes, you are possibly going, "Wow," and questioning, "Will I really experience all of these processes while reading this book? Do I really have to become aware of all of these processes?" My response: it depends how far you want to go, and you will already have varying degrees of awareness of all of these areas.

The I Make a Difference process will help you navigate these processes, and the more attention and focus you give to yourself, internally and externally, then the more familiar you will be with each of them. You will explore each of these areas on your adventure, developing your ability to recognize them, know them, understand them, and work with them so that the outcomes you experience are even more beneficial for you.

One step at a time.

Processing

Here is the magical word that goes with the process— processing.

Processing is your experience of the process. It is the movement and operation of these processes and how you deal with what you are experiencing.

Your processing is influenced by how you were conditioned to work with each of your processes. When you experience a situation that is similar to one you had in the past, any impacts from that previous situation that have not been dissolved will be triggered within you, and you will experience the processing as you did in the past. Your processing will potentially be different from that of others.

When I was blamed for things I was not responsible for, I would fight back, this is what I learnt. My internal processing involved my mental process saying, "Fuck them! How dare they!" and I would make up stories in my head filled with horrible things to say to the person. Sometimes these words would come out of my mouth or my fingertips, meaning I would send reactionary emails and texts. My emotional process involved anger boiling and raging within me, my heart beating fast, my body heating up, and my breathing becoming shallow. My energy was rapidly moving about my body with the rage and power I was feeling. My physical body went into fight mode, staunch, aggressive with a really evil look in my eye, and my fists clenched.

For another who gets blamed for things they are not responsible for, their processing may be completely different, depending on their conditioning. Their mental processing may involve them doubting themselves, telling themselves they are wrong and that it is their fault. And lots of self-talk, self-punishment, and what-ifs. Their emotional processing would include feeling guilt for being wrong, a knot in the stomach, a feeling of wanting to be sick, and a lump in the chest. Their energy may crawl into a little ball within themselves as they want to hide and be swallowed up. The physical processing results in them putting their head down, feeling their body deflate inside while holding tension under the surface of the skin and tears welling up. They might end up apologizing for something they did not do.

Both of these reactions highlight how the same trigger situation can result in different processing depending on an individual's conditioning. This is something we'll explore more in later chapters.

These are the types of processing experiences to look out for on your adventure. And as the healing and dissolving happen, you will experience the processing of your beautiful and amazing aspects and the true you.

A Note on Your Experience

Whatever you experience with your processing is what you are meant to feel, think, and experience. None of your processing is wrong. You are experiencing it, and it is surfacing within you because it is meant to. The moment you make it wrong you are rejecting your processing and yourself, and this will limit your ability to heal and grow.

You are only given what you can handle at the time. The processing that is surfacing is happening because you are ready to work with it and explore it.

Your acceptance of your processing is critical. This requires you being able to say to yourself, "I surrender, and what I am feeling is what I am meant to be feeling because if it wasn't, I would not be feeling it."

Be aware of letting go of any resistance or fight you have to what you are experiencing internally. Relax into it and be gentle with yourself, mentally, physically, and energy-wise, in the experience. Only you can give yourself permission to accept any aspect of yourself.

Expressing your processing externally is important so that you are not holding the emotions, energy, and words inside yourself. If you keep the processing inside, then it will recycle and not be released and processed through.

If your processing becomes a little overwhelming at times, where you find it feels like an overload, make it OK to take one step at a time. You can take time out and say to your system, "Please make this manageable for me," and come back to what you were exploring at a later date. It is like having a pit stop or a rest before resuming your journey.

When and how you process out your emotions, energy, and thoughts are important, as you do not want to take it out on yourself or others. The next section of this chapter offers some essentials for your adventure to assist you to do this.

ESSENTIALS FOR THE ADVENTURE

Your adventure time is getting closer. Here are the essentials to pack in your luggage to take with you:

- Support contact
- Notebook and pen
- Free writing
- Self-facilitation

Support Contact

If in your processing, you require some support in what you are feeling and exploring, then identify someone you know who will listen to you without judgement and who will support you without telling you what to do. Rather they guide you to find the answers within yourself. I do know you will only experience what you can handle; however, we all need someone to talk to and share with sometimes. And as I said, if things get a little overwhelming, have a pit stop and a rest.

Paper and Pen

In chapter 1, I gave you some questions to spend some time exploring in a journal, notebook, or the IMAD

Personal Processing Workbook you might have downloaded. As you progress through the book, what assists with your processing is to continue to use the journal, notebook, or workbook, and jot down your thoughts, memories, questions, feelings, and processing as it arises. This is why a paper and pen are an essential for your adventure.

Capturing your processing at the time it surfaces supports you to process out and release the feelings, thoughts, questions, and energy so that you are not holding onto them. If you hold onto them, they can impact what you are reading such that you find you are not entirely in your process with the book.

You will have opportunities to work with the memories and processing you have captured in the self-facilitation activities throughout the book, and the approach to take with them is one of free writing.

Free Writing

Free writing is where you pick up a pen and paper, and write down every thought, feeling, and speck of processing that goes through your head, being, and system. I sometimes refer to this as capturing and then downloading your processing.

When you free write, do not think about what you are writing or are going to write. You are capturing everything that is going on inside of you while experiencing it.

If your head goes blank, write down, "My head has gone blank." If you change subjects, start swearing, or find you are getting physical sensations, then write this down.

When you free write, it does not have to make sense. It's as if you are watching a movie of your processing and capturing the script and action. The reason for writing it down is to get it out of your head. That way you release it so that it is free from your subconscious and conscious mind.

You will find that as you free write, you explore more and more of your processing. What you have suppressed in your subconscious mind surfaces, so you consciously work with your process. You get distinctions on things, you discover further depths to your processing, you see reasons for things, and you even find that you can create a clear space to experience silence and quiet in your head.

Free writing involves writing and writing until the words and processing run dry. Next I encourage you to tear your paper from your journal and rip it up. From here you can either recycle it or burn it—responsibly, safely and only in burn season, of course. The purpose of doing this is so that you release the processing. It is a symbolic form of your being willing to let it go. Be conscious of honoring and respecting what you are releasing as it has been a part of you up till now.

Disposing of your freewriting and releasing your processing has beneficial reasons. Free writing that is focused on layer experience processing and the downloading of the mental, emotional, and energy impacts supports the unravelling and healing process of the past. The more you write out, the more you download the stories and conversations that took place allowing for more space to see things for what they were rather than what you were conditioned to see. Free writing that explores beautiful aspects of yourself supports your growth and development. By being conscious of these beautiful aspects of yourself, you connect more strongly to these parts of yourself, take greater ownership of them, and integrate them more into the expression of who you truly are.

Releasing what you have written then puts the responsibility on you to own what you have explored and released, rather than relying on the piece of paper to remind you.

If you are not ready to straightaway let go of what you have processed, make this OK. When you are ready, you will know the right time to release your writing.

If you read what you have written, you have not let it go and you may absorb some of your processing again. If you find yourself reading your free writing, ask yourself, "Why do I need to read this?"

If you hold on to what you have written, you are still emotionally holding on to the processing, the person, and the situation. Ask yourself, "Why am I holding on to this?"

Sean, a gentleman who attended an IMAD program, shared that he did lots of journaling after his wife left him. He still had the journals a year or so after the separation, and he had not been involved with any other woman since. In his process of saying this, Sean realized he was still holding onto the marriage. Upon returning home, he burned all of the journals to let his wife and marriage go. This was a significant step in Sean's healing.

Many IMAD participants take free writing on board and find that when they toss and turn at night, worrying about things, free writing out what they are processing assists to download their processing, so they can go back to sleep.

Even free writing for a minute can help shift what you are processing and be of benefit. If you find yourself in a situation where it is not appropriate to free write you can also say to your system, "I accept you are there, and I choose to process you out when I get home." Then your system will work with you as long as you keep your word. When you get home, free write out the process from earlier that day.

Free writing out what you are experiencing does not mean you are healed of that situation immediately. It supports the process of letting go of the past and your emotional attachments to it so that you can move to the next stage of your process.

As you progress through the book, you will have many opportunities to apply free writing in response to the self-facilitation activities in the chapters. These are activities that enable you to explore your processing in relation to specific areas of your healing and growth and in response to specific questions. This is why it is important we now explore what the self-facilitation activities involve.

Self-Facilitation

Facilitation is an approach that focuses on process and processing. It is about making it easier to make progress in the process and processing of the process.

Self-facilitation is applying a facilitation approach to yourself internally where a part of you is in the facilitator role asking yourself questions to work through any internal processing you are experiencing.

In self-facilitation there is a part of you that takes a neutral and objective approach to questioning the part of you that is processing and experiencing emotions, feelings, and thoughts to explore, understand, and work with your processing. You facilitate yourself in parenting, healing, and reclaiming of all the different parts of yourself and each of the emotionally aged yous from each of your layer experiences.

Self-facilitation supports you to identify what is happening to yourself and why, so you know how to work with your process more objectively.

To assist you in developing your ability to self-facilitate, you will regularly find self-facilitation activities throughout the book. These activities are comprised of questions related to the area that is being explored. You will ask yourself the questions and then free write your responses.

Let's take a rest stop, so you can explore a self-facilitation activity. Remember, the objective is to assist you in being familiar with and aware of your processes and processing.

Self-Facilitation Activity—Your Internal Processes

In your notebook or IMAD Personal Processing Workbook, free write your responses to the following questions to explore the processing you experience in your processes. If you need to review how free writing works, please do so. Also, if you'd like to download the workbook, you can access it here. Visit http://bit.ly/imadppworkbook to download.

Your Internal Processes

Mental Process

Explore the process that goes on in your mind. Consider any pictures, words, feelings, and processing.

1. Describe what your mental process is like and the processing that goes with it—what you experience, how it feels, what it looks like and sounds like.
2. Describe how you process information in your head. When you are listening to or reading something, how do you process the information—in words, pictures, feelings?

Emotional Process

Explore the emotional processes you experience. Consider the emotions, sensations, changes in temperature, energy, and physical changes.

1. Describe your general emotional process. What do you experience and how does it feel?
2. Describe the emotions you generally feel.

3. Describe the processing you experience with each of the emotions you feel. What do they feel like, look like, and sound like?

Sensory Process

Explore the sensory processes you experience. Consider changes in energy, vibrations, hearing, taste, smell, and touch.

1. Describe your sensory process and processing. What do you experience? What does it feel, sound, and look like?
2. Describe the senses you are most aware of and explore why.

Physical Process

Explore the physical processes you experience. Consider aches, flexibility, muscle memory, bodily functions, tightness, and headaches.

1. Describe your general physical process and processing. What do you experience, how does it feel, and what do you notice?
2. Describe your physical processing when you feel emotion.

Energy Process

Explore the energy processes you experience. Consider changes in energy like feeling drained, energized, tired, blocked, light, or heavy.

1. Describe how your energy is generally—what you experience, how it feels, and what it looks like or sounds like.

2. Describe what it is that impacts or changes your energy.
3. Describe your energy process when you are feeling emotion.

Spiritual Process

Explore the spiritual processes you experience. Consider what spirituality means to you and how it is experienced and expressed within you.

1. Describe what spirituality means to you and why.
2. Describe the internal spiritual process that you experience. What do you notice, how does it feel, and what does it look and sound like?

The key areas for you to shine your light and focus on are your internal processes. You have direct influence over these areas. These are the areas for healing, enhancement, change, growth, and development that impact everything you experience outside of yourself.

The more interested you are in your processes and processing, the more you will gain different distinctions, discoveries, and insights about yourself, and it can be fascinating.

Your background work to the I Make a Difference process is now complete. You are resourced with what you need for your adventure, so now it is time to embark on the next stage of your exploration of yourself. Your opportunity to delve into the I Make a Difference Onion Model is what unfolds in the next chapter.

Remember, the IMAD Onion Model outlines the process for how you came to be where you are at in your life, what you are looking for, and the details of the terrain ahead.

CHAPTER 4

THE IMAD ONION MODEL:
THE CREATION OF YOUR LAYERS

When I meet Katherine, she feels like a fragile broken bird even though she has a bright beaming smile and warm embracing energy. She experienced a workplace injury that left her with a significant reduction in hand movement, pain in her body, and what was perceived as limitations in what she could do in her life. She is living on her own, struggling to make ends meet, and locking herself up behind the door of her home.

Katherine had run her own business, had been married, had children, and once lived a very active life. She then got divorced, was injured, and chose to close her business.

She had become very disempowered in her life and at the mercy of others making decisions for her, so she wanted to remain invisible. Even though Katherine believed she had given up on what her future could be, she still had the light of hope in her eyes and the heart that things could be different.

Oh, how the situations of your life can impact you, not just externally but most significantly—internally.

As is in Katherine's situation, the key to starting to work with the impacts of experiences from your life lies in understanding the process of how you became who you are: how you were impacted in your conditioning, internal processing, behaviors, emotions, and thinking. As shared in the previous chapter, your adventure into the processes you are involved with and your processing is your focus now.

Specifically, the process of the I Make a Difference Onion Model is what you will explore in the coming four chapters. The first phase is understanding how you became who you are today and the experiences that contributed to you creating the layers you live with, which resulted in you becoming disconnected from who you truly are and your jewel within. That is what we will look at in this chapter.

Who You Are Born As and Are

Humans need a context and reason to do things—a why. Most people look externally for their purpose. However, if you have an internal purpose, then what you do externally you can achieve with greater clarity and intent, and the outcome will be more impacting.

You have the most amazing opportunity while you are in physical form *to grow and evolve and become who you were born as and are*. An internal purpose for being. You can be the true essence of what being human is all about, rather than continuing to live as the person you have been conditioned to be, the you that lacks in self-worth and hurts.

Why are you not who you were born as and are?

In the ideal world, every human being is born a beautiful being, a beautiful jewel—precious, pure, grounded, resilient, transparent, unique, and natural. You are born with all the qualities and attributes that reflect the uniqueness and goodness of being human. There are no layers, and you are the real you.

You see these qualities and attributes in little children and babies. The things you love about them that you aspire to have, connect to, and express. Adults love being around children as they feel emotionally safe, accepted, and free.

Children are the reference point of your natural state and what lies at the core of you. This is who you are born as and are:

Freedom
- free in your expression, verbally and physically, doing what is right for yourself and the right thing

Curiosity
- asking why, wanting to understand, exploring, and fascinated with things and the world

Innocence
- not conditioned, seeing the simplicity of things, living and focusing on the moment

Vulnerability
- being transparent to yourself and to others, showing the truth of what you feel and who you are

Truth

- speaking the truth or your truth, when it is right, without judgement

No Judgement

- stating things without opinion, taking time to understand and see things and people for who they are

Acceptance

- accepting what happens, accept people for who they are, accept what is meant to be

Love

- naturally expressing and sharing your love, in your looks, touch, words, and hugs

Hugs

- hugging when you feel like it, expressing yourself physically

Touch

- a curiosity to see what things feel like, touching to form connection and for/to comfort

Openness

- open to what is happening, what is shared, and to the people and things around you

Understanding

- wanting to understand others, wanting to know why things happen and how they happen, taking time to listen and explore

Gentleness

- softness and tenderness, taking a gentle approach in movement and tone, quiet and unobtrusive energy

Strength

- physical and emotional resilience, clarity on what is right for yourself, standing by what you believe is true

Expression

- free (and responsible) expression of yourself emotionally, mentally, physically, and energy-wise

Individuality

- comfortable in who you are and owning your uniqueness, knowing what is right for yourself

Sharing

- willingly offering to others, enjoying what you have with others

Receptive

- readily receiving help, love, care, support, and gifts from others

Kindness

- sharing warmth and love with others in a look, an action, a word, and just being

Trust

- trusting yourself as to what you know is right for yourself and the right thing

Awareness

- consciousness of yourself, others, what is going on around you, and what is not tangible

Happiness

- happy in who you are, enjoying what you are doing, and making the most of everything and everyone

Sense

- picking up on the intentions, energy, and processing of other people

The qualities and attributes that each of us are born with are many more than these. And yet, if we are born with all of these qualities, attributes, and more, then:

- How many of them do you feel inside of you now?
- How many of them do you express on the outside of you now?
- How many of them do you experience others sharing with you?

You will probably respond, "Depends on who I am with," which means that it is conditional, as it is based on who you trust and feel safe with.

You might even say, "Oh, I remember being curious, but I don't know what happened to that side of me." Or "Cuddles—I don't do that, that's girls woosy shit." I bet you and everyone else were cuddly when they were little.

You might even think, "Freedom—I lost that a long time ago."

You have not lost any of these amazing qualities and attributes. They lurk within you, waiting for you to see them, feel them, and give yourself permission to own and express them.

What you did was lock away inside yourself some of your amazing qualities and attributes. You stopped expressing them, stopped feeling them, and suppressed them, totally, partially, and/or conditionally.

Katherine was an example of this. Even in her emotional and physical pain, I could still see the beauty of the qualities within her. Her childlike laughter, her curiosity, her caring, her generosity, her interest in people, the love she shared in her words, energy, and approach. Only one thing missing—she could not see and feel what we could in terms of her amazingness.

All of these amazing qualities are still sitting within you. They are just waiting for you to reclaim them and tap into them and express them in your natural way, rather than your conditioned way.

As we explored in chapter 1, you will have a memory of a moment, an hour, a day, or some period of time when you were younger, where you felt and saw these qualities in yourself. Where you felt everything was right and safe, where you trusted yourself and you were you.

If you can find a photo or a picture in your head of yourself as this child, it will provide you with a visual recollection of these qualities and support you in reconnecting to these parts of yourself.

As you continue reading, if you have memories being triggered, know that this is natural. What can assist you to focus on what you are reading and exploring is to write your memories down. (This was part of your preparation for your adventure, something we explored in the previous chapter.) You can capture these in a notebook or in the IMAD Personal Processing Workbook. You then don't put any pressure on yourself to remember the memories while you are reading. If you choose to, at a later time you can work through them with the tools the book will supply you. There are opportunities to do this specifically in chapter 8. And all you have to do is refer back to what you have captured.

As previously shared, if you want to contact me to share questions you may have or your processing, or if you are interested in one-on-one personal processing sessions, I welcome you to contact me:
melinda@imakeadifferenceimad.com and
www.imakeadifferenceimad.com.

These qualities and attributes are who you are. They impact how you communicate, how you behave, how you interact with others, the energy you put out, and how you live your life. You have so much unexpressed potential within you. So many more amazing things to feel, share, and experience.

Imagine how much more love you could feel, share, and receive. The kindness that would be part of your life. The understanding and acceptance that would be a part of your home and relationships.

Layering and Conditioning

What was it that happened that removed, disconnected, and separated you from these aspects of yourself? Why are you not fully connected to them, or feeling and expressing them?

Experiences happened starting from a young age where something in your environment sent you a message that it was not OK to be who you are. This beautiful human being you are WAS NOT OK. A situation happened where you did or didn't do something and people judged and rejected you, and as a result, you put a layer up around yourself. You changed who you were, how you behaved, and how you expressed yourself in order to fit in, to be liked, and to protect yourself from being treated the same way again because it emotionally hurt. As a result, natural elements of you started being suppressed and you created a layer.

Layer 1—you might have been that child that reached out to share a hug. This was natural for you. However, the person you were with dismissed you, expressing they didn't have the time or that they did not want to be disturbed. Their response sent you the message: "Don't reach out and give hugs because I will get told off and that emotionally hurts. Wait until people come and give me a hug, it's safer."

At this point, your natural desire to cuddle and express physical connection started being suppressed. You created a layer.

Layer 2—as a child, you may have played in the mud. Your love of adventure and freedom was part of who you were. However, you got told off for getting your clothes and yourself dirty. The message sent to you as a child was

"It is not OK to play, be adventurous and free because if I do, I get told off and this emotionally hurts. Keep my clothes and myself clean, neat, and tidy."

Your natural curiosity, sense of adventure, and freedom of expression started to be suppressed and shut down. You create another layer.

Layer 3—as a child, your mother's best friend was someone you really trusted. You knew her well, you sensed what a good person she was and had personally experienced what she was like. Then your mother and her friend had a falling out. And whilst you were out shopping with your mother, you see your mother's now ex-friend. The first thing that you want to do is to run over to her and connect with her. However, your mother pulls you back and firmly states, "Don't go near that woman. She is a bad person."

You pause and hear your mother's words and feel yourself becoming confused internally. You trust what you feel about your mother's ex-friend. You also trust her as you know she is a good person. If you don't listen to your mother, do what she wants, and trust her, then you will get told off, and that hurts.

So from this point on you stop trusting yourself and start becoming reliant on trusting others' words and processes. In this case your mother's. Fearful that if you don't, you will get told off and that emotionally hurts. You create another layer.

Layer 4—during your initial school years, you are that inquisitive, curious child that wants to understand. You ask lots of questions, especially the why question. Your teacher tells you off in front of the other children, telling you to stop disturbing the class. The other children laugh.

The message that is sent to you as a child was "Don't ask questions because I get told off and others laugh at me, and that emotionally hurts." So you stop asking questions. You suppress your curiosity and inquisitiveness, and if you have questions, you answer them yourself in your own head. You create another layer.

The sad thing about this situation is that the question children ask the most is WHY. The moment they suppress this they lose sight of the purpose, relevance, and intention of why they do things, why things have happened, and the why of life. This then sets people up to do things because they are told to, rather than seeing and being motivated by the reason for them to do it. So much potential is lost.

You turn into a teenager who experiences further situations that result in you creating a layer, and this continues into adulthood. Experience after experience continues to happen, sending a message that it is not OK to be who you are. Conditioning after conditioning happens. And you either create new layers, reinforce existing ones, or add layers to your already existing layers.

This is just a snapshot of the types of impacting situations you may have experienced as you were growing up and how the past can still have an influence on your life now. These layer experiences could even be influencing you in what you are reading right now and how you are interpreting the information.

Experience after experience messages are sent, saying, "It is not OK to be who you are," so life becomes filled with layers. Until one day you either take the proactive or reactive approach.

- ◆ *Proactive approach*: you decide you really do want to sort out some of the things you feel and experience. So you say to yourself, "I know there's more to me." And you start questioning and searching for who you are. You may go bush for a period of time for reflection. You may go overseas to find out who you are. You could read self-help books, watch YouTube videos, or attend courses to discover more of who you really are. Or you could do all of the above. You take a proactive approach to working with and on yourself.

- ◆ *Reactive approach*: a crisis happens that pushes you to address what is going on inside yourself. You lose a job, a relationship ends, you get hurt physically, or some other process triggers what is lying in the layers. For Katherine it was her injury. The memories, emotions, processing, and impacts from the layers that you have suppressed start to surface. You implode internally and potentially explode externally. What you have suppressed internally affects you physically, mentally, and emotionally. You do things externally that impact you and others. You can end up depressed, sinking into the emotions and the layers and not knowing how to come out. You can fall apart, cry a lot, get angry, and flip in and out of different emotions. You can withdraw from life and lock yourself away. The cap has come off, and you are being called to face yourself, heal yourself, and change how you process and live your life so that you can uncover and discover the jewel you are. You experience a reactive approach to working with and on yourself.

You do have a choice: the pathway of the proactive approach or the reactive approach. Which do you choose? Do you resource yourself to know how to handle situations and processes that could be a hiccup or crisis? Or do you take the uncomfortable route and have the process control you?

The Layer Process

Oh, those onion layers. They hide you from yourself, and they hide you from the jewel that is within you. The more layers you put up, the more distant you are to yourself, the true you.

How close do you allow people in to see who you truly are? How close do you allow yourself in to see who you truly are?

Again, you might answer, "It depends on who it is." You only feel safe to allow the people you trust to get close to you. The chances are though that you don't show them all of who you are. You might allow others to see more of who you are than you do with yourself. Katherine was a beautiful example of this. Most people keep some level of distance from themselves and between themselves and others.

If you are doing this to yourself and the people you love and trust the most, what are you doing with everyone else? You are wandering around with your layers up, keeping yourself protected from others and them from you. Actually, you are keeping yourself protected from yourself.

You will move in and out of your layers, depending on your level of emotional safety. The movement can happen during a conversation, an hour, or a day. It is totally influenced by who you are with, what the situation is, and how you are feeling.

You may allow your children and partner close to you. When you are around them, the number of layers you have up is minimal because you trust them and feel safe with them.

However, they only have to look a certain way, use a certain tone, voice, or word, and/or act in a particular way that is similar to your experiences from your past layer situations. Next your unhealed emotion from that layer will be triggered inside you. You will have an internal emotional reaction. You won't feel safe, and you will push them right out and away from you. You will have your layers do the reverse of dominos. Up they go, one at a time as quickly as possible, so you are protected emotionally.

The interesting thing is that in doing this, you are actually distancing yourself further from yourself. You are protecting yourself emotionally from yourself. Then over a period of time—it might be a minute, an hour, a day, a week or even years—you allow them to get close to you again. You drop some of your layers. The more you trust, the less you need protection. As you are getting close again, you are on high alert. You are looking for that look, that tone, that word, or that behavior again. You are scanning for situations from those layers to reoccur. And if they do and you have emotion triggered, you push the people or person away and distance yourself emotionally again to protect yourself.

Then the process of getting closer happens all over again. And round the roundabout, we go again.

There are people in your life you may never allow close to you. There are people I have met who never drop their layers. In fact, one of them combined all of his layers so that it was like a steel vault. The hurt he had experienced resulted in him being completely distant from others and himself.

You may find when you are at home, you operate from layers closer to your jewel because you feel safe and comfortable. You are able to be yourself. Then when you go out, you put your layers up to protect yourself. Or you may find that being at home requires more layers because it is not physically and emotionally safe.

Thickening Layers

Where you experience situations that are similar to previous layer experiences, your layer will be reinforced. The layer is thickened, and you create layers within the layer. The need to protect yourself from these types of situations grows in strength. You experience a repeated pattern of situation and outcome. And your conditioned emotional reaction to this situation is what contributes to it becoming a pattern. Let's explore this using previous layer example 4.

In this earlier example, as a child you are told off at school for asking questions. The following year you have a new teacher. You pluck up the courage to ask questions. The new teacher tells you to be quiet and stop disturbing the class. Wow, this message is now doubly imprinted in your conscious and subconscious mind: "Don't ever ask questions again because I get told off, others laugh at me, and it emotionally hurts."

The message is reinforced. You make sure that that layer is really, really thick. There is no way you are going to ask questions again, as that is twice now you have experienced this. This layer is reinforced, and the unravelling of the conditioning will take some processing.

Know that you can dissolve sections of those layers. It can happen when you have supportive and constructive experiences and outcomes. For example, say that you as that same child have a new teacher the following year. The teacher takes time with you, gets to know you, and builds a relationship with you. The teacher encourages you to open up. And you feel comfortable to start asking questions again. You learn to trust and feel safe again. You allow a segment of your layer down to this teacher, as you don't need to protect yourself with them.

In the above scenario, you only lower your protective layer with this one teacher (and any other person similar to this teacher in their looks, energy, and approach). You open up when you feel safe, accepted, and that you are not going to be judged. And as you journey through life and encounter more situations where you could ask questions, you will continue to only lower your protective layer with people similar to this teacher. With everyone else, the layer of protection stays up.

At Each Layer

At each one of your layers you suppressed aspects of yourself, protected yourself from hurt, and created personas to fit in and be liked. Let's explore in depth each of these approaches you took with you.

Personas—have you noticed the people you know behaving differently depending on who they are around and what they are doing? Their expressions, the way they dress, the way they talk, the words they use, and even their laughter and smiles may be different. And you sometimes wonder which face they show is the real them.

Personas are the different faces and the different yous that you show yourself and the world from each of your layers. They are the masks, fronts, and facades you wear. Your personas are not the true you. They are the conditioned yous from each of the layers. Some people call it—the different versions of you.

When you experienced the situations that created your layers, the messages sent to you were "It is not OK to be who you are." In turn you changed how you behaved, how you expressed yourself, what you said, and possibly even how you looked. You did this to protect yourself from being judged, rejected, and so that you did not hurt again. Each time you did this, you created a persona, a new version of you. This was so you could fit in, be liked, accepted, and loved, and so you could get attention and feel emotionally safe and secure. You didn't want to experience these layer situations again.

Katherine described one of her personas like this: "I developed a survival mechanism that whenever family or friends offered help or asked me how I was, I would say, 'No, that's OK. I'm fine thanks, really I'm good'. I was far from fine or good. I was not aware at the time that I was suppressing my truth and fiercely holding onto the only thing I believed I still had left—my independence."

I met Rod, a gentleman who came across as an intellectual—academic, aloof, and serious. Rod was even called a snob. He appeared stiff, rigid, and upright. This was his external being – the persona he was showing at the time. As Rod grew his understanding and trust of himself, his childlike playfulness came to the fore. His beautiful, caring, loving, sharing, and warm self shone through. Who Rod truly was began to emerge.

To clarify—personas are not wrong. Personas are not negative. Personas are very valuable in that they help you get through life. They are necessary to protect you, while you are not aware of who you truly are, what you truly are capable of, and not trusting yourself.

If you have a persona up, yes, it means you are not the true you, and it has impacts on you that are limiting. They prevent you and others from seeing your true self and keep you removed from your truth and your jewel. They require energy to maintain them. If you do have a persona up, do so with awareness and make a choice to do so, then you will take responsibility for the outcomes you experience.

Personas are a form of protection. As at each layer you also protect yourself from yourself.

Protection of Yourself—the mere fact that you have put up layers implies protection. In protecting yourself, you pushed things down to put your walls up. The layers became your walls of protection from judgement, rejection, and ultimately emotional hurt from others. They are your protection from yourself, your emotions, your truth and hurt.

You also protected some of your amazing qualities and attributes because they were judged and you didn't want them to be made wrong again. You will do anything to avoid situations that are similar to past layer experiences. The reason being, if you do end up in similar situations, the emotions and mental processing will be triggered, and it is painful. And if you do not know how to manage the emotions and deal with what you are experiencing, you can be scared you are going to fall apart. The creation of these layers also involves you pushing down and suppressing aspects of yourself.

Suppression of aspects of yourself—when you were judged in that first layer situation you went into hiding. You suppressed and hid some of your amazing qualities and attributes. You pushed and locked them down inside of yourself. You suppressed either a degree of or the entirety of a quality and attribute as it was made wrong.

It was not just your qualities and attributes though. You also suppressed the emotions you felt at the time—the hurt, rejection, vulnerability, powerlessness, shame, guilt, abandonment, and any other emotion you felt that you expressed as a reaction to the layer situation.

In the layer situation, you may have been told in response to your showing emotion, "Toughen up," "Get over it," "Big girls/boys don't cry," or "Anger is a bad thing." You may have even been threatened, "If you don't stop your crying, I will really give you something to cry about." You may have experienced being punished for expressing the emotion, getting hit, ignored, or sent to the "naughty room." These messages communicated to you, "It is not OK to show emotion." As a result, you suppressed the emotion to cease being judged by the people around you.

The words and actions in the layering situation get imprinted on your subconscious mind. When a future situation occurs that triggers these emotions, you start feeling them again and having the same thoughts and words going through your head that you had in the previous layer situation. So you suck the emotions down and suppress them again, waiting for them to surface at another time.

Oh, how suppression impacts your life, for example:

- You don't see, feel, or express the natural amazing qualities and attributes that make you who you are. You miss out on so many amazing experiences and opportunities.

- You don't express yourself to the fullest degree; you don't experience love, adventure, freedom, and the other qualities to the extent you deserve to.

- You don't maximize having fulfilling relationships, both sharing and receiving the beauty of who you are.

- You have a lot of unhealed emotions that are just waiting to be triggered, and you are easily impacted by other people and situations.

- You keep repeating the same patterns and processes of behaviors, reactions, and situations in life due to the unhealed emotions and conditioning.

- You give your personal power away to other people and things. And you make other people responsible for your emotional well-being and decision making.

- As an adult, you look to other adults or even your children or other young people to be your parents. For them to give to you what you did not receive when you were growing up. Understanding, reassurance, acknowledgment and love, to name a few.

♦ You give others the ability to influence your life rather than you taking your personal power back and trusting your own decisions and choices.

Katherine identified how she had been impacting her life once she found the safe place to start looking at her layers and what was within herself. She was determined to find a way back and through to reconnect to herself and her jewel within.

Now that you have been introduced to the process of how your layers form, thicken, and even create layers within a layer, as well as the personas, protection, and suppression that you experience at each layer, the following chapter explores the behaviors, approaches, and processes you are conditioned in to preserve your layers.

CHAPTER 5

THE IMAD ONION MODEL: PRESERVING YOUR LAYERS

During the first day of our I Make a Difference program, Katherine considers the whole room, noticing the tables, chairs, flipchart stands, and where she expects the facilitator—me—to be. She puts a lot of thought into her position in the room. She decides to sit at the end of the group, believing she can hide, avoid having to speak, and not be noticed at all. She wants to keep herself invisible—thus maintaining that layer. Little does she know that she's sitting in the seat that has the most eye contact and attention from me and where she's the most visible.

What you learned from the people and the environments you grew up in conditioned you and entrenched the processing attached to each of your layers. You learned from others what was acceptable and not acceptable in your behaviors and approaches, in what you say, think, act, hear, and see. Also how you should treat yourself, how you should treat others, and how you deserve to be treated.

Your conditioning was driven by the need to protect yourself emotionally, which contributed to you suppressing your amazing qualities and emotions. You learned and developed certain behaviors, approaches, and processes that you applied with yourself and others in order to keep your personas in place and maintain your self-protection and emotional suppression.

The behaviors, approaches, and processes you learned to preserve your layers include control, self-talk, what-ifs, expectations, judgement, avoidance, and denial. This chapter involves exploring each of these so that you understand how your layers were formed in order to gain insight into what you do to preserve them and learn what is required of you to unravel the layers, heal the processing attached to the layers, reclaim your personal power and choices, and be who you were born as to live from your jewel within. To deepen and broaden your awareness and understanding of your processing in each of these areas, self-facilitation activities are available for your exploration in this chapter.

CONTROL

You have recently had someone very special to you leave your life. You find yourself in a public place where music is playing. The music reminds you of this person, and your emotions begin to surface. What do you do with your emotions?

You swallow them back down in your throat, tense up your face so the tears don't well up, think about something totally different to distract yourself, and get far away from the music and the public, so you don't feel what you are feeling.

We are so scared of allowing our natural process to unfold. Why? We don't trust we can handle it, we don't trust we won't fall apart, and if we do fall apart, we don't trust we can put ourselves back together again. We don't trust that things happen for our benefit. We don't trust we can be who we are and show our truth because earlier in our lives, others made it wrong and then we made it wrong. We do not trust ourselves.

The first and most significant, ingrained, dominant, and powerful behavior, approach, and process that keeps your layers and personas in place, which you learnt, is control.

Take a moment while you are reading and ponder on a time you experienced controlling yourself or where you were being controlled. Focus internally. What does the control feel like? What are you experiencing? What is the process of control?

Control is about rigidity, limitation, pressure, restriction, and manipulation. It is where you are forcing something to happen that is not naturally happening. Or you are trying to stop something from happening that is naturally happening. Then you get the people who control to have power over others. This is a key indicator of how vulnerable and emotional they are if they have to do this.

During the program, Katherine's posture exuded control. She would sit erect and upright, with a constant smile on her face while she had pain writhing through her body. She learned to control and cover up her pain with her warm and engaging persona.

In terms of the I Make a Difference Onion Model, we are exploring the type of control that is driven by the need to control your own emotions and protect your emotional vulnerability so that you don't experience the judgement, rejection, and hurt of the past layer experiences again.

In the context of the type of control that is driven by emotion, what is it you try to control?

You endeavor to control yourself, others, your environments, situations, and the outcomes you experience.

Participants I have facilitated often tell me, "Melinda, if I let go of control, I will go out of control." In response, I explain that being out of control is another form of control. You are wanting to avoid what is happening in your life, and more to the point, what you are experiencing internally.

The alternative process of controlling is managing. Managing yourself, your process, and processing rather than controlling and suppressing it. Managing involves being conscious of the process that is happening both on the inside and outside of yourself. You work with what is naturally happening. In the example scenario I shared at the beginning of the section on control, where the tears surfaced you make conscious choices as to how you will respond to them. Possibly you choose to cry, so you allow the tears to flow then and there, and it is OK. Possibly you choose to go somewhere private to cry because at the stage of growth you are at, this is more comfortable for you. Or you choose one of the other proactive approaches that we will explore. The important thing to focus on is making a choice because then you are influencing the outcome you want to experience. You are taking responsibility for your process, processing, choices, and actions, and in doing so you are doing right by you and honoring the stage of growth you are at and your truth in that moment.

How many times during your life are you told to control what you do, what you say, and how you express yourself? How many times do others want to control you, dominate your decision-making, behaviors, looks, and beliefs? How many times do you want to control others so that they do what you want so that you can feel emotionally safe and secure? How many times do you hold yourself back from doing or saying what you want?

We control because we are scared. We are scared of going out of control. We are scared of feeling the emotions and physical sensations, thinking the thoughts, and remembering the memories we have been suppressing. We are scared of ending up in situations that are similar to the ones from our past layers. We don't believe we can handle any of it. And we don't trust the outcome.

We control ourselves. We control our bodily functions, how we look, what we do, our memories, our emotions, our thoughts, what we say, and what we eat and drink. And these are just a few of the areas we control.

We also endeavor to control others in what they do, how they look, and what they say. All the same, things we try to control in ourselves, we try to control in others. And in response to our control they may react or submit and even feel diminished in their self-worth. Because when we endeavor to control others, we are saying that we do not accept or love them for who they are.

Then when others try to control us, we can get angry, control back, and even rebel. Some people will submit, give in, and give their personal power away to the other person to keep the peace or out of fear of losing the person.

If these are just some of the impacts of others endeavoring to control us, then what are the impacts on the people we try to control? If you are controlling in any way, then this means you do not trust yourself. You don't trust you can make the right decisions. You don't trust that the outcomes you experience in life are for your benefit. To let go control and manage what is happening to, for, and around you means you have to trust yourself and your ability.

Control is not a bad thing. It is not wrong. You have needed to control because you didn't know a different way. Please do not judge it as wrong or negative (remember the core belief in chapter 3: nothing is negative; it is your judgement). If you do judge it, then you are rejecting the control in yourself, which means rejecting a part of yourself. In turn, you will only reinforce a layer or layers, and reduce your receptiveness, willingness, and ability to work with your control.

Control has impacts that are limiting. It is a protection mechanism that you've utilized to keep yourself emotionally safe and secure. The more you grow your trust in yourself, the less you will need to control, the more natural your life will be, and the more you will be true to yourself and the true you.

Rest stop: the following self-facilitation activity is an opportunity for you to grow your awareness of the influence control has in your life, so that you can work toward releasing it and dissolving elements of your layers.

Self-Facilitation Activity—Control

In your notebook or Personal Processing Workbook, spend time free writing your responses to each of the following questions. With free writing, you write and write and write out your processing, and you don't question the words. Be aware of not thinking about what you write. Keep writing until the process runs its course.

Controlling yourself:

   a. What are the things about yourself that you control?
   b. What are the things in your environment you like to control?
   c. Why do you control these aspects of yourself and your life?
   d. How does your control impact you?
   e. What are you protecting yourself from?

Controlling others:

   f. Whom do you like to control?
   g. What is it about them you endeavor to control?

    h.   What is the reason you control these aspects of others?

    i.   When you've tried to control someone, how has it impacted them?

    j.   What are you protecting yourself from?

Others controlling you:

    k.   Who are the people in your life that endeavor to control you?

    l.   What aspects of you do they try to control?

    m. What do you believe is the reason as to why they try to control these aspects of you?

    n.   How does their control impact you?

    o.   What are they protecting themselves from?

SELF-TALK

Kimberly, who is important to you, promised to contact you at a certain time, but she didn't. You start feeling anxious, you start wondering what has happened. You have emotions surfacing, your mind starts processing, and the chatter going on in your head starts absorbing you. "Why has Kim not contacted me? Has she got an issue with me? Doesn't she like me? Have I done something wrong?" You even begin to make up your own stories in answering your own questions. And on and on it goes. This is your self-talk.

In the above scenario, there can be a number of reasons as to why Kimberly did not contact you. And the reason is more than likely not what you have been playing out in your mind.

Your self-talk can occur in so many situations—buying a car, going to a job interview, going shopping, driving to work, sitting exams, and even going out to a friend's place. Self-talk is noise that can be constant and persistent.

Self-talk is a form of control, which is the reason it is the second behavior, approach, and process we're exploring in this chapter. It is the mental expression of the control you experience in relation to yourself and others.

Self-talk is the voice or voices in your head. And the words and feelings that accompany each of the layer situations you have experienced. Self-talk is either:

- The words, statements, and stories that others have said to you, or
- The words and/or stories you have made up to fill in the gaps of what, how, and why things happened

At each of the layers, there is an "emotional you" stuck at your age when the layer situation happened. It's the boy or girl in you that was impacted emotionally, mentally, and in other ways. These parts of you have stories and words attached to them about what happened in the situation. They are stored in your subconscious mind.

The moment you are around a person from a past layer, an individual who is similar to a person from a past situation, or a situation that is similar to a past layer situation, the self-talk attached to that layer will be triggered. And it will come to your conscious mind. In that moment, your self-talk will influence how you treat yourself, how you feel, how you see things, what you hear, and how you behave. As well as how you express yourself, the choices you make, and your ability to react or respond.

The aim of your self-talk is to protect you from your emotions and yourself, and most significantly, to protect you from experiencing again what you experienced in the past layer situations—the judgements, rejection, and hurt.

Although it aims to protect you, your self-talk is not coming from your jewel, your truth, and your knowing. It is not your pure talk. It is your conditioned chatter. You will experience your self-talk putting you down in order to reinforce your lack of self-belief and self-worth. It will endeavor to keep you small and invisible, as was the case with Katherine. Or it will try to boost you up to do things that you may not want to do or that you believe you can't do.

It is also your gap-filler. If you don't have the information and answers, your self-talk will fill in the information based on your past. Your self-talk is your tape recordings, your inner critic, your chatterbox, and gossiper. Self-talk just jumps into your head and goes on and on and on. It can keep you awake at night, as it is the voice of your worries and concerns. It can distort your reality, as it wants to find evidence to reinforce itself.

Self-talk is identifiable by the emotion and judgement attached to the thoughts, words, and conversations you experience in your head.

James grew up with his mother introducing him to people by saying, "This is James, and he is shy." The impact these words had on James travelled right through his adult life. He would go to functions where he would want to meet people. However, the voice in his head would say his mother's words, "You can't. You are shy"—the opportunities James missed out on.

You can heal your self-talk. However, if you tell it to shut up, you are suppressing it. Oh and boy oh boy, will it come back louder and stronger.

The emotional boys or girls inside you from your layers that the self-talk is coming from, these parts of you have already been rejected; that is why they exist. You rejected them and left them behind inside yourself. They weren't listened to, and you didn't listen to them, so they want to be heard. Do not make your self-talk wrong, similar to how you are making these parts of yourself wrong too. In doing so, you reinforce the rejection you have already experienced.

Make it OK that it is there. The boys or girls inside you are talking to you, and they want to express themselves. Through suppressing them when you created the layer, you suppressed their expression. To heal yourself, you can support them to have their say through listening to them objectively, processing out their messages through writing, or verbalizing all that they are saying and reassuring them. Once they have nothing more to say, and the emotion attached to the layer is healed, they become quiet because they are accepted, loved, and integrated into who you are today.

The fact that they (the younger emotional yous) could not express the emotion at that earlier time and that they were not listened to, this is why you have those stored words and stories. If the words and stories they share came from other people, then the self-talk is not yours. Give yourself—and the boy or girl inside you from the layer—permission to let it go.

The more conscious you are of your self-talk, the more you can talk through what this part of you is experiencing and feeling to support your healing, and you can parent the boy or girl in you from the layer. Free writing is the most powerful way of working with your self-talk, so keep writing and writing to download the self-talk and get it out of you.

If you hold it in your head, you will only recycle it. Rip up your free writing or burn it responsibly and safely in burn season to release it.

<u>Self-Facilitation Activity—Self-Talk</u>

In your notebook or Personal Processing Workbook, spend time free writing your responses to each of the following questions.

a. What are the situations and who are the people you experience self-talk about?
b. What does the self-talk say?
c. How does the self-talk impact you in what you are feeling and what you do?
d. What aspects of yourself do you experience self-talk about?
e. What does your self-talk say about you?

f. What are the layer situations where the self-talk originally comes from?

g. How do you feel about yourself when you experience this self-talk?

h. If you act on the self-talk, what do you do?

i. What is the outcome of you acting on your self-talk?

WHAT-IFS

When Kimberly, who is important to you, doesn't contact you at the time she said she would, the emotions you feel attached to your self-talk result in you reacting. Your reaction is to send her an emotional message. The outcome of that is not a good one. So, your self-talk has now become questions, what-if questions. "What if I didn't send that message? What if I just waited? What if I didn't get emotional?" Oh the turmoil! How you beat yourself up and regret . . .

What-ifs are a mental process with emotions driving them. They are a form of self-talk loaded with control, and this is the reason why they are the third behavior, approach, and process that preserves your onion layers.

There are two different types of what-ifs, past what-ifs and future what-ifs.

1. **Past what-ifs**—where your focus is on what you have done and what has happened to you from a moment ago to as far back in your life as your processing goes

2. **Future what-ifs**—where your focus is on what might or could happen in the next moment stretching as far as you want into your future

We will explore both in this section.

Past What-Ifs

Past what-ifs include:

a) Regrets and lost opportunities where you did or didn't do what you knew was the right thing to do and the right thing for you

- *Example*: people who knew on their wedding day they should not get married, and yet they still did.

b) Past decisions where you did do what you knew was the right thing for yourself; however, you are making it wrong and not accepting it. This could be influenced by what other people said to you about what you did.

- *Example*: you put your hand up to accept the redundancy package being offered because you knew it was the right thing for you. However, others judged you for doing so, projecting their emotional insecurities on you, so you now question yourself.

c) Things you are grateful for that happened that you don't believe you deserved

- *Example*: someone comes along and helps you out when you are in trouble. They were right there when you needed them. And you question, "What if they hadn't been there?"

d) Past decisions that you made that were right for you and you were surprised by yourself. You listened to, trusted, and acted on your knowing. You can't believe you did because you doubt your ability to do so. If you believed in it and yourself, you would not be questioning it.

- *Example*: On the day of the wedding, the person who knew they should not get married calls the wedding off. They then question themselves about what might have happened if they had gotten married.

Past what-ifs are what could have been, should have been, or might have been if you had made different decisions and choices. "What if I had done this?," "What if I had said that?," "What if I hadn't done that?," "What if I hadn't said that?," "What if I had finished school?," "What if I had gone to university?" As well as, "What if I hadn't married that person?," "What if I had taken that job?," "What if I was born in another country?," and "What if I was born in another generation?" to name a few.

You cannot change your past, you know that. You cannot even change what happened a second ago. The past has gone. However, you can change your emotional attachment to the past.

While you have unresolved and unhealed emotions attached to past situations from your layers, they are influencing how you are feeling right now. Your past what-ifs influence how you see things now, how you feel about things now, and how you approach things now. Your past what-ifs become future what-ifs. Then you are scared of making the same mistake again.

Why Have Past What-Ifs?

There are three main reasons for these past what-ifs. In a past situation, either:

1. You did not do what you knew was the right thing and the right thing for you. You did not listen to, trust, and act on your knowing. You emotionally reacted and did something you regret. OR

2. You went against what was important for you. You made decisions to please other people. You fulfilled other people's expectations of you. Your decisions were influenced by your emotional neediness, vulnerability, and lack of self-worth, as opposed to your jewel and your knowing. OR

3. You did make the right decision and had good things happen to and for you. And due to your lack of self-belief and self-worth, you don't trust your ability to make the correct decisions, and you don't believe you deserve good things in your life. So you struggle to own the wonderful things you gained from the decision you made and the experience you had.

I was offered a position with a large organization in the UK, which involved spending six months training in the USA. This was a dream opportunity for me. I turned it down. At the time my neediness to be with the man I was with dominated my processing and decision-making. That relationship only lasted for about seven months. I experienced many regrets and what-ifs about not taking the opportunity of the position in the UK. I struggled accepting the choices I had made. My emotional neediness dominated my knowing and truth. What if I had made different choices? Where would my life have journeyed to?

Managing Past What-Ifs

In brief, download and process out the emotion from the past, from the layer. Learn from the situation, come back to now, and put that learning into action.

From now on, always do what you know is the right thing and the right thing by and for you. Where good things have happened to you, you deserve them. Embrace and own them. Listen to, trust, and act on your knowing, which is you trusting the answers within you and the decisions you make. As you progress through this book, the approaches, processes, and self-facilitation activities support you to grow your trust and love of yourself.

Bring your focus and attention back to what is happening currently, what is going on at this moment, and make the most of life and living in the now. Right now is the only space where you can make decisions that influence what happens to you in the next moment and your future.

Future What-Ifs

There are two main future what-ifs:

1. Hopes, dreams, obsessions, fantasies, and desires. Your emotional neediness to be safe and secure. "What if I win the lottery?"

2. Your fears, anxieties, concerns, and worries. Your vulnerability and emotional neediness to be safe and secure. "What if they leave me?"

Oh, how your future what-ifs can absorb every part of your being. What a wonderful fairy-tale world we can live in, or a suspense movie.

Future what-ifs are where you question what might happen, could happen, or should happen in your future. You are driven by the fear that you will repeat the past layer situations again. Or you feel powerless to change your future and are dreaming of a miracle or at least something to save you. Including prince or princess charming.

Your future what-ifs are driven by emotion, and they are based on your past what-ifs and experiences. They also can have been created as a result of other people telling you what they believe will happen, and you buy into their belief, for example: "If you take a sick day, you will get the sack" or "Apply for this job because I know you will get it."

If you have future what-ifs, then you have some part of yourself living in the future. How can you interact with people fully, how can you do what you are doing effectively, and how can you concentrate with future what-ifs occupying your headspace? You are not fully here.

The only way you can influence your future is by focusing on what is happening now and making conscious, proactive decisions to influence the outcomes you experience.

Managing Future What-Ifs

In brief, work through your worst-case scenario of what might happen. Download, through free writing and/or verbalizing, the emotion and fear you are experiencing and ask yourself, "What can I do if this happens?"

There is always something you can do, so determining it will bring you back to looking at the practicalities. Come back to now and ask yourself, "What can I do now to influence the outcome of the situation?," "What are my responsibilities in this situation?" Then where appropriate take action.

When you proactively work with future what-ifs, you are able to dilute the hold that the fear has over you, and you become the influencer of what will happen.

Rest stop: the following self-facilitation activity will support you to dissolve the emotional grip your past and future what-ifs have on you and your life.

<u>Self-Facilitation Activity—Past and Future What-Ifs</u>

In your notebook or Personal Processing Workbook, spend time free writing your responses to each of the following questions.

   a. List and explore any past what-If questions you may have or have had.
   b. What are the reasons why you have these past what-if questions?
   c. What is the influence and Impact they have on you?
   d. What can you learn from them?

e. List and explore the future what-if questions you may have or have had.

f. What are the reasons why these future what-if questions are in your head?

g. How are the future what-if questions impacting and influencing you?

h. What actions can you take to address the future what-if questions?

i. What is the impact of your what-if questions on how you treat and feel about yourself?

EXPECTATIONS

You find yourself in a similar situation to what you have experienced in the past. Paul, another important person in your life, made a commitment to contact you at six this evening. As the time gets closer to when the contact is to happen, you start experiencing a familiar energy you may not fully recognize. Your self-talk kicks in and future what-if questions begin to surface. You start assuming that Paul will not contact you. And as your emotions begin to dance inside you, you get worried you are going to get rather emotional about it all and feel let down. What are you expecting? What are your expectations in this scenario?

And then Paul contacts you.

So much energy you use up on this, so much time taken up, how absorbed you become, and how exhausted you can feel.

Expectations come in many many different forms. How you know you have expectations is that you will have an emotional attachment to an outcome.

Expectations are loaded with what-ifs, and they focus on the situation, experience, and outcome. They are your way of controlling yourself to keep yourself protected and suppressed from hurt and pain. They are the fourth conditioned and impacting behavior, approach, and process you apply with yourself and others to keep your layers preserved.

Be mindful not to confuse expectations and responsibilities. There is a fine line between them; however, they are different.

Responsibilities are tasks and commitments that you are required to fulfil based on the choices you make. For example, you choose to take on a job, and there are tasks you are to perform. These are your responsibilities. An example of this is if you have children, you are responsible for keeping them healthy and safe.

How you go about performing these tasks and responsibilities can be influenced by your expectations, which are driven by emotions, for example, "I've got to get it right, I've got to get it perfect, I am going to stuff it up." Expectations come about when you put pressure on yourself to perform.

Yet how do you define what is right, perfect, or a stuff up? They are standards and measures you try to live up to or down to, such as, "I have to be the best, or I am going to be useless." These standards and measures come from society's and others' beliefs about what is right and wrong, what is acceptable and not acceptable, what is success and failure.

Consider these expectations: "Men are the providers," "Women are more emotional than men," "Burping in public is rude," "You should say excuse me when you sneeze," and "Baby boomers work harder than Millennials." Then there's: "You should do this, you shouldn't do that, you must be . . ." . . . . Enoughhhhhhhhh. Who originally said these things?

Expectations are also where you live out the unlived lives of your parents or grandparents. This is where parents push their child into activities, sports, jobs, or study so that the child can achieve what the parents didn't achieve. And the child ends up living their parents' life, not their own.

Expectations are also the scripts you write in your head before speaking to someone or going into a situation. You predict what is going to happen, what is going to be said, and how things will unfold. Why? You want to keep yourself emotionally safe and secure because you don't want to experience again what you experienced in the past when it hurt.

You have expectations of yourself, others, situations, and outcomes, and others have expectations of you.

Expectations put so much pressure on you. You end up disappointed that you haven't, or others haven't, met your expectation. You can also be surprised because your expectation has been met or exceeded, and you can't believe it.

Katherine had the expectation of being able to live independently, and her injury impacted this. Living on her own, she found it physically difficult. Opening jars or cans proved impossible, and she struggled with housework and shopping. Her workplace rehabilitation and disability employment services provider conducted an independent daily living assessment for Katherine. The results of the assessment were confronting, and she was not comfortable. Katherine refused to accept assistance because she believed it meant she was letting go of her independence, as it would undermine the expectations she'd set for herself.

With conforming to or rebelling against expectations, you don't live the life that is right for you. You live your life based on what society and others want of you. You don't accept the wonderful things you deserve, and you can be stubborn. All in the vein of holding onto your beliefs that protect and suppress you, rather than dealing with practicalities.

When you expect certain things to happen in situations and life, your focus is on your expectation and what will happen in the future. This diminishes your ability to embrace and enjoy what you are experiencing in the moment and your ability to have new wonderful experiences. Your expectations do not allow you to be who you really are or others to be who they truly are when with you. You do not express the potential within yourself. You don't see the true you; instead, you look for evidence to satisfy your expectation boxes to keep yourself emotionally protected.

Rest stop: your expectations of yourself impact you mentally, emotionally, energy-wise, and physically. The following self-facilitation activity supports you to identify these impacts, so you can release the hold they have on you.

Self-Facilitation Activity—Expectations

In your notebook or Personal Processing Workbook, spend time free writing your responses to each of the following questions.

   a. What are the expectations you have of yourself?
   b. How do these expectations impact you and your life?
   c. Why do you have these expectations of yourself? Where did they come from?
   d. What are your expectations limiting you from experiencing?

JUDGEMENTS

Cynthia has been saying unkind and unfair things about you. You feel the emotions welling up inside. You feel the hurt of being disrespected, unfairly treated, and even betrayed. Then your self-talk starts up, and you begin to judge her. You imagine sharing what you are thinking with Cynthia in the quest to hurt her back. Then as the intensity of the emotions you feel subside, you start to judge yourself as you feel the impacts of what she said.

Judgements are the most hurtful thing you do to others and to yourself.

Judgements are a form of you controlling yourself by punishing yourself and/or you trying to control others by punishing them. Judgements are a form of self-talk loaded with emotion, so they are the fifth behavior, approach, and process you express to yourself and others that support the layers of your onion.

When you make a judgement of someone or something, you are making some aspect of them wrong. You are rejecting them and not accepting them for who they are, and you are not accepting what happened. Judgements are opinions and views. Your opinions that are driven by your emotions and desire to protect yourself, fit in, be accepted, and be emotionally safe and secure. Judgements can be vicious and nasty—gossip, backstabbing, racism, sexism, ageism, bitching, put-downs, criticism, sarcasm, ridicule, and stereotyping, to name a few.

When you judge others, you are projecting and dumping your own self-judgement onto them. You have emotions and self-judgement going on inside yourself that you don't want to deal with and own. You are judging yourself. When you judge yourself, you make yourself wrong, put yourself down, and reject yourself. Haven't you already had enough of that in your life without doing it to yourself? You reinforce the judgement and the very layer that the judgement originally came from.

Your self-judgements reinforce your self-doubt that you can't do something or do it well enough. They reinforce your lack of self-belief that you should not trust yourself and you don't have the qualities and attributes that others have. And your lack of self-worth that you don't deserve wonderful things because you are not good or worthy enough.

Peer group pressure is an excellent example where judgements get played out. I have spoken to a few people who have made rude comments about someone, but they don't actually mean them. They are just joining in with the group because of their emotional need to belong.

Bullying is where the bully is judging themselves; however, they take it out on others to run away from their own self-judgements in an effort to make themselves feel better. It doesn't work though, as the issue lies within them.

When you judge other people, it is not just your words and behavior directed at the person; it is also the energy attached to the emotions that you are feeling that gets directed. People feel this energy, and it can be powerful. In fact, you don't even have to have verbalized the judgement; even you just thinking it will direct the energy at them.

When you judge another person, you can hurt them. You can reinforce their lack of self-belief and lack of self-worth. They may even take on board your judgement and believe it is true, so they then judge themselves, as was the case in the scenario with Cynthia at the beginning of this judgement section. Remember that what you put out you get back. Don't be surprised that if you judge others, you get judgements back.

If you judge yourself a lot, you may find that the judgements you get from others is a reflection of what you are doing to yourself. Take responsibility for your own self-judgement. Own your issues and work through these, rather than dump and project them onto others. In judging yourself, you are judging the emotional boys or girls in yourself from your layers. Instead, work on connecting with them and accepting them and all aspects of yourself. They are you.

A situation that really impacted me in relation to my judgements was where I was running late to a meeting and generally I was a stickler for being on time if not early. As I was driving to the meeting, I started going off in the car about the driver in front of me, calling them useless and many expletives. I heard what I was saying and ceased abusing them. This driver was driving at the speed limit and doing everything right. I asked myself "What am I judging about me?" I was angry at myself for running late to the meeting. It had nothing to do with the driver in front of me. I was projecting and dumping my expectation issues and emotions on them.

Allow yourself to peek behind your judgement wall and see the beauty in yourself and others. Take time to understand rather than judge. This will support you to grow your acceptance of yourself and others. Be kind to yourself; then you will be kind to others. And you potentially will receive more kindness back.

Rest stop, the following self facilitation activity is an opportunity for you identify the judgements you have of yourself, so you develop your understanding and acceptance of who you are and in doing so be kind to yourself.

Self-Facilitation Activity—Judgements

In your notebook or Personal Processing Workbook, spend time free writing your responses to each of the following questions.

    a. List the judgements you have and make of yourself.
    b. How do these judgements impact how you view, feel about, and treat yourself?
    c. Why do you have these judgements?
    d. What are you not accepting about yourself?

AVOIDANCE

Remember Cynthia, that person you had a falling out with, that treated you unkindly that we mentioned in the previous section about judgement? Well, as you are walking down the street, you suddenly find her walking towards you. You start feeling things physically as you tense up, and you want to vanish into thin air. Your emotions race through your body, and your self-talk starts going manic with expectations of what is going to happen and what-if questions are firing on super blast. OMG, what are you going to do? What do you do?

Runnnnnnnnnnnnnnn!!!!

Avoidance—we gotta love the process . . . Avoidance is your conscious denial. "My what?" you might be asking. Yes, that question shows even more avoidance. Before I clarify what I mean here, welcome to your sixth behavior, approach, and process that you have been conditioned with.

As you can see, when you avoid, you are totally controlling, and all of the other behaviors and processes come to the fore with it. Avoidance exemplifies the extreme lengths you may go to to keep your personas in place and keep yourself protected and suppressed.

This is all because you are avoiding what is going on inside of yourself: your emotions, your responsibilities to yourself, and your truth. Duhhhhh and wow. Quite simple, really.

What are the tasks at home you have been putting off? Who are the people you have not returned calls or emails to? Who are the people you don't want to see or hear from? What are the physical things you have not addressed? Which phone calls do you not answer?

Avoidance. The art of putting off, delaying, deferring, handballing, skirting the issue, procrastinating, and an array of other tactics you have armed yourself with.

Avoidance is where you are conscious of what you don't want to deal with, so this is why I call it "conscious denial." It is where you have your blindfold and ear muffs partially on to enable yourself to be selective in what you want to see and hear.

So, why does anyone avoid? More importantly, why do you avoid?

You may answer, "To avoid confrontation," "I can't be bothered with them," or "I will get to it when I have time."

Justifications for avoiding are another tactic of avoidance.

When you face someone you are avoiding, it is not the confrontation with the other person you are avoiding; it is the confronting of your own emotions and issues. You may be scared you will lose it, fall apart, get angry, and potentially even do something you know isn't right. You can also be worried about how you will feel if you share the truth with the person and the what-if about them feeling hurt.

Your avoidance is not about the other person. It is about you. Your avoidance of yourself. You don't want to face yourself, your vulnerability, and self-judgements. Why? You don't like the feel of that, and you don't know how to manage it.

Katherine was talented at avoiding. During the program when she received attention and beautiful feedback, she would deflect the focus to others and acknowledge them instead of receiving what was being said about her. She was avoiding hearing the words being spoken because of the lack of self-worth she felt inside, as she did not believe she deserved the acknowledgment she was receiving.

You know the longer you leave addressing what you are avoiding, the worse it gets. Your ability to influence the outcome you will experience is reduced. You give away your personal power to the other person or situation. You give others the ability to influence the outcomes you experience in your life. All because you don't want to face what is within yourself.

The tooth that needs a filling, and it turns into an abscess—your fear of the dentist because of past experiences, and you may not want to admit you do not have the money to go to the dentist. Your avoidance results in it being more costly, more painful, and your choices as to what you do about it are reduced.

The bill that you have not paid—you are avoiding admitting both to yourself and the power company the financial situation you are in. Your power gets turned off, and the bill ends up in a debt collection agency. There goes your credit rating, and you get hounded.

The lawns you haven't mowed, which turn into fields of long grass—you are avoiding admitting you don't want to mow them, and you're avoiding asking for help or asking someone else to do it. You are avoiding being judged, being reliant on others, and possibly even being useless in your own eyes. When that mowing does happen, it takes twice as long and is twice as tiring.

The tasks you put off at work—you end up with a written warning, or even worse, you're sacked because maybe this is not the first time.

We are experts at taking simple things and making them into the most complex mountains that are taller, wider, and harder to climb than Everest.

This doesn't even take into account the impact the avoidance has on you or on others. Paranoia, suspicion, lots of self-talk scenarios you make up. Worst-case future what-if scenarios that would make a great movie. Your conscious mind worries about what you are avoiding, and you write a script of justifications for not addressing the person or thing. You expect the worst, and like a suspense movie, you judge all the characters that are in your plot, including yourself.

So much energy used. And so much time put into avoiding, thus impacting so many areas of your life.

Face what you are avoiding in yourself, your emotions, your self-judgement, your vulnerability, and your truth. Work through your future what-ifs and your worst-case scenario. Download the emotion and fear. Then if required, go and face the situation or person so that you get to influence the outcome you experience. I know that this is all easily said and a bit of a process to work through.

Rest stop: when you cease avoiding and face what you do not want to address within yourself and where relevant outside of yourself, you take back your personal power. You take responsibility for yourself and you have a greater influence on the outcomes you experience in your life. The following self-facilitation activity provides you with the opportunity to explore your avoidance, so you can take these steps.

Self-Facilitation Activity—Avoidance

If you want to skip and avoid this one you can—LOL. In your notebook or Personal Processing Workbook, spend time free writing your responses to each of the following questions.

    a. List the things and people you are avoiding.

b. Identify what the true reasons are as to why you are avoiding them. Be gentle with yourself when you are doing this.

c. How is your avoidance impacting you? Consider the impact on your mental, emotional, energy, and physical levels.

d. What is it in yourself that you are avoiding and not facing?

e. How does your avoidance impact how you feel and treat yourself and your life?

f. What would happen if you stopped avoiding these things?

DENIAL

I ask you, "You know Cynthia, that person you had issues with, the one you explored in the Avoidance and Judgement sections?"

You respond, "Cynthia? I have no idea what you are on about. I haven't experienced any avoidance or judgement issues with Cynthia. My relationship with her is fine."

Ahhhh, denial. This is exactly what denial is—where something does not exist, it didn't happen. You have shut it out and shut it down, locking it away in your subconscious mind. It is unconscious avoidance; you are avoiding but are not aware you are doing it. Your earmuffs and blindfold are now doing their jobs. You are blind, deaf, and numb to something.

You may be relieved or not, as denial is the seventh and last behavior, approach, and process that keeps your personas in place and keeps you protected and suppressed. Denial is where you have applied extreme control and suppression to shut out what you are in denial about. There is a likelihood that you will have shame and guilt attached to your denial. You do not want to feel, see, or admit it. You can even create a new reality when you are in denial and live in la-la land.

You can be in denial about your relationships, other people, situations, work, business, finances, objects, and outcomes. You can especially be in denial about yourself. Denial of your emotions, your amazing qualities, and your health. As well as what you have done or said, your past, and any other aspect of yourself and your life.

Denial requires so much control to keep it locked down, so it often takes a crisis of some form to come out of denial. A traumatic experience that shakes you into consciousness and out of denial. A crisis, such as a disease, a death, a relationship breakup, or a job loss. Also loss of your business, a financial crisis, and emotional breakdowns.

Denial is not just about the things that are not working in your life; you can also be in denial about the good things in your life. The wonderful aspects of people, situations, relationships, and outcomes. Denial about the amazing qualities that make you who you are, your knowing, your value, and your worth.

I have not included a self-facilitation process for denial because if you have denial, you don't know you are in denial. If you are interested in exploring denial then I encourage you to get support to do so if relevant.

You can ask yourself, "What is it I am not seeing in myself? What is it I don't want to admit to myself?"

If you get no answers, then leave it alone. If you get answers, then you know what to work with: either healing the areas from the layers or reclaiming and owning the good things about yourself.

In this chapter you explored the protective behaviors, approaches, and processes that you have been conditioned to do to preserve your layers. By recognizing when you are operating in these ways, you can unravel and release them, so you can address what lies beneath them: the aspects of yourself that you have suppressed. As such, it would not be surprising that you may be feeling some vulnerability about the possibility of letting go of those familiar and ingrained behaviors, approaches, and processes. That would be completely understandable.

To let them go, it involves taking one step at a time. Also it requires you to trust yourself. You will need to rebuild that trust in yourself, so you can trust that you can work with your process and that you will be OK. The key is to remind yourself that your reason for doing this is to reclaim yourself, the true you, and connect to the jewel within.

As you release your conditioning, what you have protected yourself from and suppressed within yourself will surface, especially the emotions that lie within your layers. It's those emotions that the next chapter focuses on.

CHAPTER 6

THE IMAD ONION MODEL: INSIDE YOUR LAYERS

When I first meet Katherine, she can not say the word "crap." The control she has over her emotions and the expression of them is significant. To feel and express emotions leaves her vulnerable to others' judgement, so Katherine smiles rather than externally show her emotions. She suppresses her hurt and anger within herself, controlling it and locking it into hard balls of energy and pressure. These caught and blocked areas of emotion and energy contribute to the manifestation of headaches, pain in her wrists, and stress in her body, as she is holding on so tightly to not expressing the emotion.

The unravelling and releasing of your conditioned behaviors, approaches, and processes covered in the previous chapter allows for the emotions you have suppressed within your layers to surface. Without your emotions emerging you cannot heal your layers.

In order to heal these emotions that you have suppressed, the important starting point is to identify the emotions and understand the process attached to each. This will support the growth of your ability to accept and embrace each emotion. These are the key elements to the next stage of this process—and this is what this chapter guides you through.

> Before venturing into the emotions, I will reiterate something really important: emotions are not negative. If you believe emotions are negative, then you will reject your emotions, which means you are rejecting yourself, and you will not be able to work with them effectively.
>
> Emotions are not bad. That is your judgement and yet again your rejection of them. Emotions are emotions. They can feel uncomfortable, painful, and wonderful. Describe them, not judge them.
>
> It is how you express the emotion that is important. The energy and words need to be externalized as part of the healing process. However, in expressing them, please never hurt others, objects, or yourself. Aim to express the emotion in a healthy way.

Suppressed Emotions

When the situation occurred so long ago that created the layer where you were sent the message, "It is not OK to be who you are," you experienced and expressed emotions. The reactions from the people around you to your emotions generally were ones of judgement and rejection. And as a result of these messages you suppressed what you were feeling because it was made wrong. As such, your emotions lie within you, waiting to be triggered by layer experiences.

There are three main ways that emotions buried and suppressed within your layers get triggered:

1. When you find yourself in a situation that is similar to one from your past layers, suddenly the suppressed emotions from that layer get triggered.
2. When you find yourself around people from the past layers and they are behaving in the same way they did back then, suddenly the suppressed emotions from that layer are triggered.
3. When you find yourself around people who are similar to the people from the past layers in their behavior, their tone, the words they use, their look, or their energy, suddenly the suppressed emotions from that layer are triggered.

When you experience the triggering of an emotional reaction, it will result in you acting in a conditioned and automatic way to express the emotion. This will result in you repeating the outcomes you want to change. Your emotions control you rather than you managing them.

While there are many emotions and they often work in rapidly changing combinations, in this chapter we'll focus on the following: hatred, anger and hurt, guilt and shame, rejection and abandonment, loneliness, and grief. For each of these emotions, you'll find a self-facilitation activity that provides you with guidance to explore and give attention to the emotion.

HATRED

People find this a strong word let alone emotion, and they are right. It is strong in its energy and how it can explode within a person. When you hate someone, what do you want to do them? You want to HURT them because you are hurting.

Hatred is suppressed and stored up anger. And anger is suppressed and stored up hurt. With hatred you have hurt that has been suppressed and locked up for a reasonable period of time that is full of caged energy, so when it is triggered, it's like an explosion through your system. There is a powerful release of energy, and it comes out as hatred. It is desperate, powerless hurt. And you want to get your power back and have the hurt be gone.

If you had been encouraged to express the anger when you initially felt it (in a healthy way) and not suppress it, it would not have built to hatred. If you had been encouraged to express the hurt at the time you felt it, it would not have built to anger.

People have scorned hatred, saying it is a bad thing. It is an emotion you can feel, so don't make it wrong. However, it is what you do with it that is important. They also say, "I 'dislike' people rather than 'hate' them." Ummm, OK, that's just controlled hatred. Hatred and dislike are similar; however, from my experience the energy behind each one is different. They are influenced by the level of suppression, degree of hurt, and who the person is.

With the people you are more emotionally attached to and easily affected by, you will tend to experience hatred due to the hurt being more impacting. If you are not as attached emotionally to the person, you won't feel the extreme of hatred, rather a lesser energy and process of dislike. In both circumstances you still feel hurt.

Being someone who expresses her processing, I have said I hate people. I have felt the hurt to the core, and I have felt so powerless in certain moments that I have wanted them to hurt like I was hurting. As I grew my understanding of what hatred was about, when I felt it, I changed how I expressed my hate. I would say, "I hate you, but I don't really, I am hurting, and I want you to hurt and that is my issue." As a result of this change, I experienced a very different outcome because I was owning my truth, rather than covering up the hurt with hate.

I don't agree with hating people. I have felt it and experienced it though, and the reality is, people do have these feelings at times. The key is being able to capture the anger before it becomes hatred. Express it in a healthy way, and get it off your chest, so you are not hurting yourself or others. Even more important is to capture the hurt the moment you feel it and express it in a healthy way. Then it won't build to anger.

ANGER AND HURT

Your expression of the emotions you feel were influenced by what was acceptable, not acceptable, and what was demonstrated in your environment as you were growing up. What you were conditioned to do, based on what others did or didn't do, and how you were treated when you felt and expressed the emotions.

In my family, we expressed our emotions through anger. We did not show hurt because it was preyed upon and seen as a weakness. You were a wimp if you showed hurt.

I grew up being very comfortable with expressing anger but not hurt. However, I expressed anger in a very destructive way. For my healing, I worked on expressing my anger in a healthy way. And I grew my ability to embrace and work with hurt, as this was unfamiliar for me.

Other people grew up feeling comfortable expressing their hurt. It was accepted in the family, but they may not have been comfortable expressing anger. Individuals may have felt scared when others in their family got angry, so they became afraid of their own anger. Or if you experienced painful consequences for being angry, then you may have suppressed your anger to avoid further consequences.

Swearing at people is not appropriate. Swearing as a release and freeing of the energy and control of your emotions, especially for people like Katherine, is a liberating process. She even became comfortable enough to say "fuck." For her this was her freedom being expressed in her speaking her truth. It does not need to be an ongoing process; however, giving yourself permission to do this when it is sitting there for you is about being true to yourself.

Why is it important to be able to access and express both anger and hurt? As we have explored, the environment you were raised in influences you as to what emotions are acceptable to express and how. So with anger and hurt, you may be more comfortable with one over the other. To ensure you are not suppressing any of your emotions, so that you can work with healing all aspects of each layer and the emotion within them, it is important you are able to express both. Also underneath the emotions are key amazing qualities that are at the core of who you truly are. I will explain.

Underneath your anger lie the qualities of self-belief and strength, both of which are key in your ability to do what is right for yourself, to believe in yourself, and to trust yourself. Heal the anger and what you are left with are the two beautiful qualities of strength and self-belief.

What enables you to feel hurt are the qualities of acceptance and gentleness. Heal the emotion of hurt and what you are left with are the two beautiful qualities of gentleness and acceptance. Combine all your amazing qualities—self-belief, strength, acceptance, and gentleness—and you are closer to who you truly are and to your jewel within.

HURT

You will know this one. Hurt is the emotional pain you feel. The emotional wounds you experience. And you can feel burned, scarred, and even broken.

Hurt is the process of giving your personal power away to another person. You make them responsible for your emotional well-being. You are dependent on them to feel emotionally safe and secure, and they can easily affect you. You are emotionally needy of them to make your vulnerability feel safe and secure.

Take back responsibility for your own emotional well-being through working with your vulnerability and you make it safe and secure. In doing so you will be filling your own neediness and will become self-reliant. Then you won't feel hurt again as you will not be emotionally dependent on others, so you won't be emotionally impacted by them.

Easily said and a bit of a process to achieve.

Rest stop: here is an opportunity to explore your processing around hatred, anger, and hurt, so you can build your relationship with these emotions for the purpose of growing your acceptance of your emotions, so you can take steps to heal them.

Self-Facilitation Activity—Hatred, Anger, and Hurt

In your notebook or Personal Processing Workbook, spend time free writing your responses to each of the following questions.

Hatred

a. If you have experienced the feeling of hatred, describe what it felt like and the process you went through. If you have not felt hatred but felt dislike, then explore this.
b. Why were you feeling the hatred?
c. How did your hatred impact you?

Anger

a. What are the things that make you angry?
b. What is the reason they make you angry?

c. What do you do with the anger when it surfaces?

d. How does your anger impact you?

Hurt

a. Who are the people that you have felt hurt by?

b. What did they do for you to feel hurt?

c. Why did this leave you feeling hurt?

d. How did the feeling of hurt impact you?

In amongst the anger, hurt, and pain, there are other significant emotions that will also surface from the layers when they are triggered: guilt and shame. Powerful emotions that can be worn like armor. They are both emotional impacts of each other and are similar in nature but are also distinctly different in their process. We'll start by looking at guilt.

GUILT

Ah, that situation you walk away from, knowing you could have done things differently. Your self-talk goes over and over in your head justifying what you did, making excuses, and even occasionally condemning you. Your stomach is eating away at you, and you try to do things to distract yourself. You may even just get busy to avoid what you know.

However, the self-talk continues, and you can't concentrate or sleep. You find yourself apologizing, overcompensating, and making up for what you knew you could have done differently. This is your guilt.

Guilt is that gnawing feeling inside you where you feel you have done something wrong. Where you feel, "I am to blame. It is my fault," and where you feel responsible.

There are three types of guilt: warranted guilt, unwarranted guilt, and over-responsibility in the guise of guilt. Let's take a moment to examine each type.

1. *Warranted Guilt*

This first kind of guilt happens when you said or did something (or not said or did something), and you knew it was wrong. You went against what you knew was the right thing to do. You didn't listen to, trust, and act on your knowing. You acted on unclean intentions, meaning you chose not to take responsibility for yourself, your actions, your words, your choices, or your emotions. You may have dumped your issues on others and even went out to hurt and upset them. You avoided something.

You are completely entitled to feel this guilt. This is your guilt, and it is warranted guilt.

2. *Unwarranted Guilt*

When you said or did something (or not said or did something), and you knew it was right, but others made you wrong and dumped their guilt and issues on you. This is not your guilt, do not take it on board, and do not carry it. You listened to, trusted, and acted on your knowing. You acted on good, clean, and innocent intentions. You didn't go out to hurt anyone, you didn't go out to not take responsibility, and you didn't go out to dump anything on anyone. You did what you knew was the right thing to do and right by you and your true self.

You will experience this type of guilt when you spoke the truth, and others did not believe you, said you were lying, and made you wrong. And you weren't lying. Do not take on any guilt about this. It could come from a time where you innocently laughed at something and others told you off and made you wrong. This is their issue they are projecting on you.

This is not your guilt. It is unwarranted guilt.

3. *Over-Responsibility*

The third type of guilt comes in the form of over-responsibility. The process that unfolds that creates over responsibility stems from when you were young, and you took on board adult-type responsibilities and behaviors, and grew up well ahead of the time you should have. You became an adult as a child. This conditioned you to you believe you were responsible for others' emotional well-being and that you had to fix, save, sort out, protect, make right, and rescue other people from being hurt. You were rescuing them from themselves, their learnings, their emotions, and the issues they were facing. And if you didn't do this, you felt guilty. You parented adults. And you may still be doing so.

You are only responsible for one person, and that is you, yourself—unless, of course, you have children. And if you do, you are responsible for your children until they reach the age where they take responsibility for themselves. For every other human being your responsibility is to treat them with respect and care.

If other people blame you for things that you know you haven't done, don't take it on board. It is not yours. You can walk beside the people you want to "rescue" and support them to take responsibility for themselves. Support them to learn, grow, and become self-reliant. If you do "rescue" or attempt to "rescue" them, you prevent them from the experiences they are meant to have, to aid them in their growth, and you are encouraging their dependency on you. So if they fall down and apart, then you are guilty because you contributed to what they are experiencing.

The following situations are examples of the conditioning that can lead to over-responsibility and the ensuing feelings of unwarranted guilt:

As a child, you may have been mum and dad to your siblings. You parented your brothers and sisters because Mum and Dad were working all of the time. Or, you may have been raised in a solo parent family where you took on board some of the roles of the parent that was not around, like cooking dinner, cleaning, and nurturing your parent who was present. Or, you may have been blamed for your mother or father's misery, and they made you responsible for what they experienced.

This is not your guilt. It is unwarranted guilt that came about from over-responsibility.

You will not feel guilt again, if you:

- always do what you know is the right thing and right by you;

- don't buy into other people's beliefs that you are wrong when you are not; and
- don't carry other people's issues, guilt, and responsibilities for them in an attempt to "rescue them," but, rather, you walk beside them.

Yes, it is easily said and a bit of a process to go through. This is why we are on this step-by-step I Make a Difference adventure together. And having time to have a rest stop to process each of these steps is why you have the self-facilitation activities, like this one.

<u>Self-Facilitation Activity—Guilt</u>

In your notebook or Personal Processing Workbook, spend time free writing your responses to each of the following questions.

a. What are the things you have done or not done that you feel guilt about?
b. Who are the people you feel guilt about?
c. Why do you feel guilt about them?
d. How does your guilt impact you?

SHAME

There are aspects of your life you don't share with people because of how you feel about those aspects and what you believe others would say. During a conversation, the topic turns to that aspect that you keep tucked away from sight. Your heart thumps, your mind races, screaming, "What if they find out?" You either change the subject, make judgements of the topic, or get up and leave while the conversation carries on. Your shame is impacting you.

Shame is where you have done something or had something done to you or where there is some aspect of you and your life that you are hiding. You don't want others to know about it because of the judgements and the stigma attached to what you are hiding.

Who are you hiding the shame from? You are hiding it from yourself. You don't want to face your own self-judgements about what you feel shame about. Denial is the behavior that is often associated with shame as you lock the shame down, so you don't see it, hear it, or feel it.

In experiencing shame, it comes in a range of impacting processing and the following are the varying degrees of shame you can feel:

Embarrassment—this is the mildest form of shame. This is where you say or do something very innocently, you judge yourself for it, and you feel embarrassed. An example: you might have a random loud burp in the middle of someone's speech.

Ashamed—this is when you experience shame about someone else. This is where somebody you are connected to does or says something that you feel ashamed about because of the judgements attached to what they said or did. Examples: you may feel ashamed of your parents fighting in public. Of the way a family member behaves. Or of your partner's employment situation.

Shame—see definition above.

Humiliation—this is the ultimate shame. This is where you share your shame with another person, they disclose it to other people, and they humiliate you. The vulnerability you exposed has been shared by another to others.

You can feel shame about nits, foot odor, bad breath, spelling ability, writing, IQ, the car you drive, and the job you have. You can feel shame about shoplifting, drinking problems, weight issues, hair color, finances, your house, and your friends. And your religion, sexual orientation, culture, skin conditions, bedwetting, marital status, age, and more.

When you experience shame and you hide something from yourself, you are vulnerable. You are vulnerable to other people finding out about what you are hiding, and then they can judge you. They only have to bring up the subject, and you start getting butterflies and feel scared.

You are hiding your own truth from yourself, and you are the one judging yourself. When you own your shame, stop judging yourself, and stop making it an issue, then what anyone else says does not have an impact on you. There is no judgement or emotion left to be triggered.

Yet again, easily said and a bit of a process to work towards. Your commitment to yourself in reading this book, having rest stops, and completing the self-facilitation activities support you to move forward on the path of the process.

<u>Self-Facilitation Activity—Shame</u>

In your notebook or Personal Processing Workbook, spend time free writing your responses to each of the following questions.

   a.   What are the things you have previously or currently feel shame about?
   b.   Why have you felt shame about these things?
   c.   What do you do when you feel shame?
   d.   How has or does your shame impact you?

The two most impacting emotions that you have inflicted on yourself from the very first layer are rejection and abandonment. They are the key emotions that prevent you from accepting who you are. They are similar in nature and yet distinctly different in their process. The emotion to explore first is the one that we often fear the most—rejection.

REJECTION

You applied for jobs and you either get an email saying you were not successful with your job application or you don't receive any reply. What do you start feeling? What is your self-talk telling you? "I am not good enough. I am a failure. I am useless. Nobody wants to employ me. I am not experienced enough."

We are so so good at rejecting ourselves.

Rejection is the process that hurts the most. Yet the only way you can feel rejected is if you are rejecting yourself. Self-rejection is you making aspects of yourself wrong and where you are not accepting them.

If you are not rejecting yourself, then what anyone else says is their opinion, their issue, and their own rejection, which they are projecting onto you. You won't be impacted because their rejection has nothing to attach to within you.

Rejection is a feeling of not being wanted, not fitting in, not feeling liked, not being loved, being irrelevant, and being misunderstood. As well as not being seen, not being heard, feeling nobody cares, being pushed away, being made an outcast, and most significantly, being made to feel some aspect of yourself is wrong.

Katherine rejected herself through trying to make herself invisible. This happened in relation to where she sat herself in the room for the program. As well in her efforts to make herself invisible by putting all of the focus of her attention on others and redirecting any attention she was given. She did not believe she was worthy or deserving of being cared about or being seen.

Rejection from Others or Your Rejection of Them

When someone rejects you, that person has issues and emotions or amazing qualities inside of them that they do not own, don't want to deal with, and are rejecting in themselves. With you being around them, you may remind them of someone from their past layers (or you are the person from the past layers), and their issues, emotions, and amazing qualities get triggered. They don't want to feel these things, so they reject you and push you away. In doing this, they can continue suppressing all that they are rejecting in themselves, again. They take their own self-rejection and project and dump it on you.

The process is the same when you reject other people. You are taking your own self-rejection and projecting it onto others.

So why do you do an incredible job of picking up other people's rejection of you and taking it on to make it yours?

The rejection others dump on you buys into your own self-rejection. At the very first layer, where you were sent a message that it was not OK to be who you were, you were rejected by others. So you did the same thing to yourself. You rejected part of the boy or girl you were at that time. In doing so, you rejected some of your amazing qualities and emotions. Then every time you put up a layer, you continued to reject yourself and make yourself wrong.

Every time you put up personas, every time you suppress your emotions and amazing qualities to protect yourself, you are rejecting yourself. And every time you control, self-talk, what-if, have expectations, judge, avoid, and deny, you are rejecting yourself. Every time you fight or resist yourself, push yourself, put pressure on yourself, or are hard on yourself, you are rejecting yourself.

Cease rejecting yourself, accept who you are, and you will never feel rejection from anyone ever again. As with the other emotions, it can be easily spoken about; however, it is bit of a process to go through.

Rest stop: time for exploration of your rejection of yourself to support you in your progress towards embracing and accepting all aspects of yourself. This self-facilitation activity takes you a step closer towards you achieving that.

<u>Self-Facilitation Activity—Rejection</u>

In your notebook or Personal Processing Workbook, spend time free writing your responses to each of the following.

    a. Who are the people in your life that you reject?
    b. What is it about them that you reject?
    c. How is this a reflection of what you are rejecting in yourself?
    d. What is it you reject about yourself?
    e. Why do you reject these aspects of yourself?
    f. What is the impact on you of your rejecting yourself?

ABANDONMENT

You are having a day where you don't feel good and you want to talk to people who are close to you for support. You phone and text each of them; however, no one answers or replies. You are left alone in what you are feeling. No one is available to be there for you. You feel lonely. Your self-talk starts asking questions about why no one has gotten back to you, and you start making up stories to fill in the gaps.

Abandonment is different and yet similar to rejection. In rejection, the focus is on you. You are the reason why the person doesn't want to be around you. In abandonment, you are not the reason.

Abandonment is where a person, an animal, or some precious object leaves you for a period of time. It could be a couple of hours, days, months, years, or for forever. They leave you for their own reasons. You are not the reason. And you miss them, you miss the amazing qualities they shared with you.

The following are examples of scenarios where feelings of abandonment can surface: the passing of a person; your parents forgetting to pick you up from school; friends meeting you for coffee, and not showing up; friends moving to another city or country; a person you were close to at work who gets a job elsewhere, and you not hearing from them; or people not responding to your messages you send them.

In all of these scenarios, the person didn't leave you because of you; it was other circumstances happening in their life. More often than not, the other person or people got busy and forgot because other things absorbed their attention, as is the case in the scenario described in the first paragraph of abandonment.

Even still, you feel left behind, home alone (a great movie as an example of abandonment), neglected, and forgotten about. You are left with lots of questions: "Where have they gone? When are they coming back?" and the biggy "Why?" And if your questions are not answered, then your self-talk will fill in the gaps. You then blame yourself and start rejecting yourself.

Why do you see it as abandonment? Why do you not just see it as that person was late, or they got busy or died, or they've gone overseas?

You see it as abandonment because you are emotionally needy and dependent on them to feel the qualities you are not feeling in yourself.

At the very first layer experience you had in your life you not only rejected part of who you were (you made a part of you wrong), you also abandoned part of the boy or girl you were. And you abandoned some of your amazing qualities. You didn't make these parts of you wrong (like in rejection); rather, you pushed them to the side and left them behind to access other aspects of yourself so that you could cope and survive in your environment.

I experienced this personally with regards to my gentleness. I don't ever remember making it wrong and rejecting it; however, I remember accessing my strength at a young age to cope in the environment I was being raised in. In accessing my strength and focusing on this for my protection, my gentleness got pushed to the side, suppressed, and forgotten about.

Cease abandoning yourself. Cease abandoning the boys or girls inside yourself. Cease abandoning what is right for you and your amazing qualities, and you will never feel abandoned by anyone ever again.

As with the other emotions, it is easily said and a bit of a process to go through. And as you cease abandoning yourself and reclaim the qualities and attributes that are you, the abundance of love, joy, understanding, and freedom continues to expand in your life. You do the things you love to do and that are right for you because you deserve to.

Rest stop: feeling abandoned by others is a reflection of what you have abandoned in yourself. This self-facilitation activity will support you to explore this and identify what it is in yourself you can cease abandoning and reclaim.

Self-Facilitation Activity—Abandonment

In your notebook or Personal Processing Workbook, spend time free writing your responses to each of the following questions.

    a. Who are the people in your life you have felt abandoned by?
    b. What did they do or not do that left you feeling abandoned by them?
    c. Why do you feel abandoned by them?
    d. How did the abandonment impact you?
    e. What is it in yourself you have abandoned?

LONELINESS

In feeling each of the emotions we have explored so far, an impact of each of them is that you will experience the emotion of loneliness. And you know you don't have to be alone to feel it. You can be in a room filled with people who are close to you, and you can still feel lonely.

It is the feeling of emptiness, where you have emotional holes that you are needy of being filled. You feel disconnected, separated, isolated, secluded, excluded, and convinced that nobody understands or loves you.

And you can focus your loneliness on the fact that you are not connecting emotionally to others.

You may turn to things like food, alcohol, drugs, partying, texting 24/7, cleaning, working, shopping, and exercising, trying so hard to fill the loneliness and distract yourself from what you are feeling.

Katherine's self-imposed isolation through locking herself in her house and refusing assistance from and interactions with anyone else was her way of running away from her loneliness and disempowerment. Through not interacting with others, she did not have the loneliness triggered, as she had no reminder of the separation from others she was experiencing.

These band-aid approaches for filling your loneliness hole will give you a quick fix. The loneliness is suppressed for a while. Then it will surface again because the healing needs to happen internally not externally.

Nothing on the outside of you will fill and heal your loneliness.

Loneliness is where you have disconnected and separated yourself from the true you. From your jewel, your truth, your knowing, the boys or girls in you, and the amazing qualities that make you who you really are. The rejection and abandonment you implemented with yourself is what facilitated the disconnection from yourself.

Reclaim, reconnect, and embrace your jewel, your truth, your knowing, the boys or girls in you, and your amazing qualities, and you will never feel lonely again.

As with the other emotions, easily said and a bit of a process to go through. Each section of this book that you progress through is movement closer in reconnecting with the true you.

The difference between being alone and loneliness: when you are alone, it is a choice and you want time just for yourself. You are valuing yourself. Loneliness has an emotional desperation and neediness to it, i.e., needing someone or something else to make you feel better. Aloneness is you choosing to be on you own, feeling quite content with it.

Rest stop and time to check in with yourself: a self-facilitation activity to explore your loneliness as you take further steps to reconnect to the true you.

Self-Facilitation Activity—Loneliness

In your notebook or Personal Processing Workbook, spend time free writing your responses to each of the following questions.

   a. What are the situations where you feel loneliness?
   b. What has happened that has left you with the feeling of being lonely?
   c. What do you do when you feel the loneliness?
   d. How does the loneliness impact you?
   e. What is it in yourself that you are not connecting to?

GRIEF

What lies cradling all of your other emotions is your grief. You know you have reached depth in your emotions when you feel it. It is the final letting go, the grieving for the loss of what was, what could have been, and what should have been.

Grief sits at the bottom of all the other emotions because when you experience grief, you feel every other emotion: anger, hurt, guilt, shame, rejection, abandonment, and loneliness. You experience all of the conditioned approaches: control, self-talk, past and future what-ifs, judgements, expectations, avoidance, and possibly some denial. Grief is overwhelming, painful, and healing. Grief is the most powerful emotion we can experience. The energy attached to it comes from deep down in the belly. Grief is mourning, deep sorrow, wailing, loss, and, specifically, the loss of.

The loss of people, the loss of animals, the loss of objects, the loss of opportunities, the loss of time and what we have done to ourselves. People do not have to have died for you to experience grief; they may have left your life and moved on.

Grief in relation to others—this is what you grieve for with regards to other people:

- You grieve for the experiences you had with them that you can no longer have with them because they are no longer around.

- You grieve for the experiences you had the opportunity to have with them but that you never took up at the time, and now they are not around.
- You grieve for the experiences you were meant to have with them but didn't get to have with them because they are no longer around.
- You grieve for the loss of the beautiful, amazing qualities they shared with you.

You can't do anything about even a second ago, it's gone. In dealing with grief, it is about allowing yourself to grieve so that you can heal. It is about expressing, processing out, and letting go of the emotional attachment to what you have lost. Then go and have the experiences that you did have in the past or that you didn't take up at the time or that you were going to have; however, it will be with different people.

While I was holding onto the grief of losing my grandfather who loved me unconditionally, I was blind to seeing and receiving the unconditional love from the people who were currently in my life.

Grief in relation to yourself—then you also grieve for yourself in the following ways:

- You grieve for the time you lost by being disconnected from your jewel, your knowing, your amazing qualities, and the boys or girls inside yourself.
- You grieve for the opportunities that you didn't take up at the time and what you missed out on.

- You grieve for what was done to you, i.e., the experiences that created and reinforced each of the layers and, as a result, what you missed out on.
- You grieve for what you allowed to be done to you and, as a result, what you missed out on. Such as: the times you stayed in relationships where you weren't treated right and you knew that they weren't right for you. You could have had time in a relationship that was right for you. The times you wanted to go overseas, but you stayed behind because your partner or whoever didn't want you to go. Now that person is no longer in your life. You stayed in jobs where you weren't treated right and that weren't right for you. And you missed out on finding or being in the job that was right for you.
- You grieve for what you did to yourself. When you did the things you knew were wrong. When you didn't value and respect yourself. When you punished yourself. When you didn't do what you knew was right for yourself.

Express the grief and know by doing so, you are loving yourself. You are honoring your process and who you are. Allow yourself to heal and embrace the learning from the process. You are letting go to allow more into your life and more of a connection to the true you. Commit to living your life and making the most of every moment and everyone.

Rest stop: a self-facilitation activity to honor the "loss of" in your life, the connections, the sorrow, and the impacts this has had on you, as you heal the impacts of your past.

<u>Self-Facilitation Activity—Grief</u>

In your notebook or Personal Processing Workbook, spend time free writing your responses to each of the following questions.

a. Whom and what have you grieved for?
b. What was it about them that you were grieving about?
c. What did you do when you felt the grief?
d. How did your grief impact you?

We have journeyed through many layers of the layers, exploring what preserves the layers, and what is within them. We delved into the behaviors and approaches we take with ourselves and others to keep our personas in place, keep ourselves protected, and keep our emotions, qualities, attributes, and true self suppressed. We have then dived beneath these behaviors to explore the emotions we have suppressed. Now we find ourselves in the place of the underlying issues: the key drivers to all of our emotions and behaviors and the source of our processing. This is what we explore in the next chapter.

CHAPTER 7

THE IMAD ONION MODEL:
THE LAST LINE OF PROTECTION

"What good are you to me? Look what's happened! You can't lift or carry, can't open the store, and can't close the store. You need to realize that your body is telling you that you can't do this sort of work. What more proof do you need? You're not going to be able to continue on here."

Upon hearing these words, Katherine feels hurt, sick, and scared. She feels vulnerable in relation to her job and being judged and rejected by her employer. She is emotionally needy to feel personally and financially safe and secure. Her value and worth become eroded by her employer's judgements and by her physical inability to do the work. This leaves her in doubt as to her ability to get another job. While at the same time her levels of trust in others, life, and most importantly, herself significantly decline.

Now for the truth of what actually influences, drives, and lies at the bottom of every one of Katherine's and your layers—the five underlying issues. They are the last bastion, the last line of defense and protection from you truly being you, reclaiming your personal power, your choices, your life, and being the true you.

As in Katherine's example above, the impacts that are triggered in you from each layer situation will include all five underlying issues. So in unravelling your behaviors and approaches, and healing your suppressed emotions, the remaining requirement is to address and dissolve the impacts of your underlying issues.

Every one of your protective behaviors and suppressed emotions include all of these five key underlying issues lurking beneath their surface. All five of the issues are identifiable individually and also intertwined in their dynamics.

At the time of the first layer experience, when you expressed in your behaviors and words your truth and emotions, and you were sent a message that you were not OK, a seed for each of the five underlying issues was planted. And as you continued to form layers, the outcomes of these meant they grew in their strength and influence.

The lack of support and understanding you experienced resulted in the creation of emotional holes, such as *neediness*. The safe space to share your truth and emotions diminished, so you became scared to expose yourself—*vulnerability*. As you were judged for what you did or didn't do, you began to doubt your ability—*self-doubt*. The rejection of your qualities and self-trust resulted in you doing the same to yourself—*lack of self-belief*. And all the messages you received were laden with "You are not good enough, worthy, or of value," especially for being the true you and you believed them—*lack of self-worth*. Every behavior and approach from your layer tracks to an emotion within your layer and what lies beneath these are all five of the following underlying issues:

1. **Neediness**
2. **Vulnerability**
3. **Self-doubt**
4. **Lack of self-belief**
5. **Lack of self-worth**

These five underlying issues collectively influence you and your life in ways that are so subtle and yet obvious and powerful in their impacts. You can unravel your conditioned behaviors and you can heal your emotion; however, if you do not take steps to work with all five of the underlying issues that are driving your behaviors and emotions, you will not fully dissolve your layers and reconnect to your jewel within. This chapter explores each of the five underlying issues to support you to recognize, understand, and take further steps to self-facilitate the healing and reclaiming of you.

NEEDINESS

Oh, how people do not like this word, let alone the process. Who wants to admit they are emotionally needy? The truth is every single person on this earth is needy and will have been at some point. So let's accept it, embrace it, and work with it. Our neediness is part of us, just waiting for us to fill it.

Neediness is where you experience an emotional lack of.

For example, when you were growing up, your parents and the other people around you were not able to give and share with you what you truly and naturally deserved. Their own onion layers prevented them from doing this. So you went without. You experienced a deficiency in your emotional well-being. This deficiency created emotional holes within you. The emotional holes that you long and yearn to fill.

In needing to fill your neediness, you turn to other people, objects, experiences, and other things to fill the emotional neediness holes. In doing so, you make them responsible for your emotional well-being. You are emotionally dependent on them, and so you are easily affected by them.

If they give you what you are needy of, you feel the fix of feeling emotionally happy and secure or you want more and more. If they don't give you what you are needy of, you are disappointed, hurt, and even angry. You are dependent and reliant on these people and things to make you feel emotionally safe and secure.

The following are examples of what you can be needy of:

- *Needy of attention*—party animals, flamboyant dressers.
- *Needy of being heard*—people you can hear a mile away, or people that mumble, so you have to get close to them to hear what they have to say. They can even say, "Did you hear what I said?" or "Are you listening?" at the end of their sentences.

- *Needy of being understood*—individuals who say, "Do you know what I mean?" at the end of their sentences, and they do this quite unconsciously. They fight to have their point understood.
- *Needy of reassurance*—individuals who say, "Is that right? Is that right?" at the end of their sentence quite unconsciously. They will share their stories with you to get you to reassure them that what they did or are going to do is OK. They need confirmation their decision is the right one.

As well are these types: being needy of freedom, acknowledgment, recognition, fitting in, belonging, being the same, being different, being special, being important, acceptance, and being respected.

All neediness processing tracks down to three key areas of neediness, and they are linked to the other underlying issues:

1. *Neediness to be of value and worth*—connected to your self-worth and self-doubt
2. *Neediness to be loved*—connected to your self-belief
3. *Neediness to be safe and secure*—connected to your vulnerability

Your neediness can suffocate people. It sets up codependent relationships, addiction, the spending of lots of money. It can leave you feeling drained and confused, or it can drain and confuse others.

You can feel pathetic and weak, and reject others' neediness, as you are rejecting your own. The emotions go to the extreme highs and lows, as you react to whether you have got what you are needy of or not. You look to the outside world to fill your neediness and emotional holes. You shop, eat, drink, work, exercise, or clean excessively. As well as text 24/7, obsessively check social media, get way too much plastic surgery, try to rescue others, and try to buy friends.

You are dependent on others to fill your neediness holes. However, no other person and nothing external can ever fill it. All of these emotional hole fillers are actually only band-aids and quick fixes.

There is only one person who can fill your neediness, and that is you. It is about you connecting to the boys or girls in yourself. You understanding yourself. You hearing yourself. You giving yourself attention, you accepting yourself, you valuing yourself, you loving yourself, and you making your vulnerability and emotions safe and secure. Then you won't be emotionally dependent and needy of others and things. And you won't be emotionally impacted by them. Instead, you take back responsibility for your own emotional well-being.

I encourage you to accept your neediness and make it OK because the moment you judge it, see it as a weakness, and make it wrong, you are rejecting yourself. Neediness is what it is. Love your neediness because it is a part of you, and one day you might not feel it anymore. This rest stop gives you a wonderful opportunity to explore and make friends with your neediness, as you work towards accepting and filling your neediness yourself.

<u>Self-Facilitation Activity—Neediness</u>

In your notebook or Personal Processing Workbook, spend time free writing your responses to each of the following questions.

    a. Describe how other people's neediness feels. For example, when you detect someone's neediness, what do you feel and experience? What is the process?

    b. What are other people needy of from you?

    c. What do you do when other people are needy of you?

    d. Why are they needy of you?

    e. Whom and what are you needy of?

    f. Why are you needy of them?

    g. What do you do when you are needy?

    h. How does your neediness impact you?

VULNERABILITY

Your neediness for safety and security is intertwined with your vulnerability. This is the second issue lying in the depths of your layers for you to embrace and work with.

When you feel vulnerable, you are scared of showing anyone your vulnerability. You are afraid that other people will see it, use and abuse it, and you don't want to experience that because it hurts.

Who you are truly scared of showing and admitting your vulnerability to is yourself. Being vulnerable is about exposing you to you. You facing your truth and being willing to look at everything and anything inside of yourself and admit it and own it. Own your judgements, your feelings of rejection, your not coping, your fear, your emotions, your neediness, your amazing qualities, and all the other parts of yourself that you have been suppressing and protecting yourself from.

Katherine had stopped trusting the world and most importantly herself. Her self-imposed isolation protected her and filled her neediness for safety and security. Her invisibility meant she was not exposed, and in particular she was not exposed to herself. This was her way of dealing with her vulnerability, as she had little trust in herself and could not face her truth.

When you see and own your vulnerability, you stop being scared of it and it becomes part of the process of owning your personal power. That's when you live from your jewel within, knowing and doing what is true and right for yourself.

However, you are conditioned to hide from and be scared of your vulnerability and to view it as a weakness. As you were growing up, the people around you—due to their onion layer conditioning—were rejecting their own vulnerability. As a child when you shared your truth and what you were truly feeling and your emotions, i.e., your vulnerability, that triggered their vulnerability. They didn't want to feel this, so the rejection process started. So to push their own vulnerability back down, they needed to reject your vulnerability and shut it down. They may have said things like "Get over it," "Don't be a wimp," "Toughen up," "Nice day we are having," or even completely ignored you.

If you experienced this, then you grew up not having any safe space where your vulnerability was accepted, respected, and honored. Instead, you potentially viewed your vulnerability as you being used and abused.

Your vulnerability was made wrong, so you made it wrong. You experienced a lack of being emotionally safe and secure with your vulnerability. So then you became emotionally needy of being safe and secure. And the moment you met someone or something you felt safe with and trusted, you became dependent on them to provide that safety, to protect and accept you. You became needy of them.

If neediness is about you filling the emotional hole, then it is about you making your vulnerability OK and safe and secure.

Vulnerability leaves you feeling scared, anxious, nervous, and having butterflies. You are emotionally naked, nothing is hiding, and you are EXPOSED. Who you are exposed to is yourself and your truth.

The moment you own your vulnerability and say, "I'm scared, I am feeling upset, or I am hurt," people can't use and abuse you because you are owning and voicing what is true for yourself. That takes great strength and self-belief. They may laugh at it, but whose issue is that? Theirs because they are feeling uncomfortable.

As a lady said to me once, vulnerability is about being scared of facing your own truth. If It Is your truth, why are you scared of it?

In exposing your truth to yourself and facing your vulnerability, as you can experience in this rest stop with this next activity, you are strengthening your ability to own all parts of yourself. This allows growth of your acceptance of yourself.

<u>Self-Facilitation Activity—Vulnerability</u>

In your notebook or Personal Processing Workbook, spend time free writing your responses to each of the following questions.

a. How do you view your vulnerability?
b. Why do you view it this way?
c. Whom and what do you feel vulnerable around?
d. Why do you feel vulnerable in these situations?
e. What do you do with the vulnerability when you feel it?
f. Why do you do this with your vulnerability?
g. In what way does your vulnerability impact you?

SELF-DOUBT

Possibly about now, you might be self-talking, "Can I do this? Can I work with all these elements of myself? Can I unravel, heal, and dissolve these layers, the parts of myself that are preventing me from being me?" If you find yourself asking these questions, then welcome to your third underlying issue, self-doubt. Self-doubt lies at the intersection of the two underlying issues that we have already explored—neediness and vulnerability—and the two you are yet to explore—self-belief and self-worth.

Self-doubt is doubting your ability to do things. It can be your ability to drive, ability in an interview, ability to do a presentation, or ability to cook. As well as your ability to be a parent, ability to manage your emotions, ability to speak your truth, ability to connect to your knowing, and ability to reclaim and express your amazing qualities.

When you experience self-doubt, you will experience many of the behaviors, approaches, processes, emotions, and all of the other remaining underlying issues we explore in the I Make a Difference Onion Model.

Let's expand on the opening example of you experiencing self-doubt about your ability to work with all of these parts of your onion. Here's how that self-doubt can play out: you will find you have lots of self-talk, "How am I going to go? Am I going to fail? Is it going to be overwhelming? Will I give up? What if I cannot cope with it?" You will have lots of future what-ifs, "What if I don't heal my emotions? What if I continue to emotionally react? What if I don't connect to my jewel?"

If you have previously been working with your personal development and you have felt you have had experiences that were limiting or impacting, then potentially your self-doubt will trigger past what-ifs, "What if I had finished the course? What if I had not gotten absorbed in what I did and instead stayed focused on myself?"

You will potentially have expectations about how you will go: "I'm going to nail this," "I'm going to be a failure. It hasn't worked in the past, so why would it work now?," or "I already do all of this and nothing is different."

You will be judging yourself, "I don't have the resilience to stick at it. I am not as strong as so and so." If you are doing all of this, then you are controlling yourself and rejecting yourself.

You will be needy of reassurance: "Somebody, please let me know I can do this, let me know that I can unravel my conditioning, heal myself, and connect to the true me."

You will feel vulnerable because you will be scared of facing some of your memories, emotions, and exposing yourself to the process, your truth, and yourself. You will also be scared of what others may say about you: "What if my beliefs about myself are true? What if people don't like who I really am and they reject me and that hurts?" So you will be emotionally needy to feel safe and secure.

You will experience a lack of self-belief as you are not trusting your knowing because your emotions are overriding it, so you can't even hear it. You don't see or own the amazing qualities and attributes you do have that are who you are, as you are wrapped up in the fear of rejection.

You will have a lack of self-worth because you believe you are not good enough, and you don't deserve to be who you truly are. In this way, you see how self-doubt brings all the parts of your onion and all the aspects of the process into play.

As with other parts of the process, owning, embracing, feeling, and working through your self-doubt is how you dissolve and resolve it. At first it isn't comfortable, but the confidence and trust you will feel from doing so makes it well worth it.

Rest stop: the following self-facilitation activity will guide you through the first steps of dissolving the self-doubt that lurks in the bottom of your layers.

Self-Facilitation Activity—Self-Doubt

In your notebook or Personal Processing Workbook, spend time free writing your responses to each of the following questions.

a. What are the areas of yourself and your life where you experience self-doubt?
b. What is it about yourself that you are doubting?
c. Why are you doubting yourself in these areas?
d. How does your self-doubt impact how you feel about yourself and what you do?
e. Where in the past does the self-doubt come from?

LACK OF SELF-BELIEF

Neediness, vulnerability, self-doubt . . . you possibly are wishing that that was it as far as the elements residing in the underlying areas of your layers. Umm—wrong.

The lack of self-belief and the following underlying issue, lack of self-worth, are critical, important, and essential both for your healing and for the reclaiming of the amazing aspects of yourself that will allow you to grow and shine.

Before exploring the lack of self-belief, you will require a reference point of what self-belief is. I am sure you are saying, "Isn't it about believing in yourself?" Yes, it is, but what is it specifically in yourself that you are believing in?

Self-belief is about:

- believing in and trusting your knowing,
- believing in your ability and trusting yourself, and
- owning and believing in the amazing qualities that make you who you are.

Why do you experience a lack of self-belief? Maybe you don't? It's a good opportunity for you to check.

During your life, there was likely a time when you were judged, potentially put down, and told what was wrong with you, and you believed it. You found you mainly received feedback when you did something wrong. And if you do get good feedback about who you are and what you do, it may be an unfamiliar experience. So you didn't receive it well, let alone hear it. People also traditionally had the belief, "If you own the good things about yourself, then you are arrogant and full of yourself," so you didn't go there.

At the very first layer of protection and suppression that you created, someone sent you the message: "It is not OK to be you." Who you truly were, the amazing qualities you expressed, and the trust you had for yourself were judged and rejected at that moment. Then and there you started to experience a lack of self-belief. Your trust of yourself started eroding, as did your belief in your knowing, so you started rejecting and abandoning some of your amazing qualities. And this process continued every time you put up another layer.

You have so much potential. You have so much beauty, strength, belief, trust, and personal power at your core. You have your jewel and yourself. The more you unravel your layers—your conditioning—and heal your emotions, the more space there is for your amazing qualities and yourself to shine through.

The more you consciously reclaim your amazing qualities and attributes, the more you trust yourself and your knowing, and the more your self-belief, self-confidence, and self-acceptance will grow. That's what this journey is all about.

Self-Facilitation Activity—Lack of Self-Belief

In your notebook or Personal Processing Workbook, spend time free writing your responses to each of the following questions.

a. What are the qualities and attributes you see in yourself?

b. What are the qualities and attributes in yourself that you don't see and own fully?

c. Why do you not see these qualities?

d. What are the situations where you trust yourself?

e. What is it in yourself that you are trusting?

f. Why do you trust yourself in these situations?

g. Why do you not trust and believe in yourself fully?

h. In what way does your lack of self-belief impact you?

LACK OF SELF-WORTH

You are here, the last of the underlying issues sitting in your layers. Lack of self-worth is one of the greatest influences on the quality of a person's whole life. As with self-belief, it is important you are clear about what self-worth is, so then you can explore the lack of it.

Self-worth is about:

- valuing yourself,
- making yourself important,
- putting yourself first,
- acknowledging who and what you believe you deserve in life, and
- believing in and owning the amazing things that you have within yourself, that you have on the outside of yourself, that are in your life now, and that you will have in the future that you deserve because of who you are.

The amazing things you have within you being your love, gentleness, freedom, joy, health, intelligence, truth, and yourself.

The amazing things on the outside of you being your family, friends, job, car, house, animals, and respect. There is no limitation on this.

You can have all of this and still feel unworthy, undeserving, and lacking in self-worth. So why?

You may have been told you have to work hard to have the good things. So if someone offers you help because they want to and you believe you have done nothing to deserve it, you get suspicious and think, "What do I have to do to earn it?" And you may not even accept it.

If you have mainly been judged and put down, then this is what you are familiar with. So when a person gives you a compliment, such as "You look beautiful today," "You are so kind," or "You are such a gentleman," the chances are you won't even hear it let alone receive it. Why? Because you don't believe you deserve it or that it is even you.

You may have been told you were useless, worthless, and this is all that you deserve. And so you start believing it.

If you weren't important to your parents, then why would you be important to yourself? If you were treated like shit during your life, then you believe this is what you deserve.

You are told, "If you put yourself first, you are selfish," so you put everyone else first.

When that first layer experience occurred, you were judged and rejected, and you started to question your value, your deservedness, and your importance. Then at every other layer experience, you continued to do so. This compounded your vulnerability in believing you deserved to be judged and rejected. This strengthened your emotional need to prove your value. Reinforced your self-doubt through you believing you did not deserve to succeed, complete, or achieve things. And contributed to your lack of self-belief because you are not good enough or worthy enough to trust yourself or be who you truly are.

The more you value yourself, the more you make yourself important to yourself, the more your respect of yourself and your self-worth will grow.

The more you know you deserve all the amazing things in your life, and you open yourself up more in making them happen and also receiving them, the more your deservedness will grow.

You are worthy and you are valuable and you deserve abundance in every way. Why? Because you are you and it is as simple as that.

Rest stop: explore your lack of self-worth, so you can identify the areas to work on growing your belief and ability to go for and receive what you truly deserve.

Self-Facilitation Activity—Lack of Self-Worth

In your notebook or Personal Processing Workbook, spend time free writing your responses to each of the following questions.

a. Around whom and in what situations do you experience a lack of self-worth?
b. What is the lack of self-worth about?
c. What is the reason why you feel the lack of self-worth?
d. What are the things you believe you don't deserve in life?
e. Why do you believe you don't deserve them?
f. What are the things you believe you do deserve in life?
g. Why do you deserve them?

    h.   How does your lack of self-worth impact you?

How the Process Unfolds

Please remind yourself that none of what you have explored is wrong or negative or bad. To do so is your conditioning of how you view your behaviors and approaches, emotions, and underlying issues. They are what you learned and are a judgement. You will only reinforce a layer and suppress aspects of yourself. You reject yourself, and you prolong your process.

As you progress with your commitment to discovering and reclaiming yourself, you will experience travelling from the outside layer of your onion, down through the layers, the layers in the layers, layer by layer, all the way to your jewel and your amazing qualities and attributes.

The process moves in and out, through the layers, and has many dimensions and processes to it. There is no one right way for this process of unravelling the conditioning, healing the impacts from the past, and dissolving your layers to unfold. Your process will have its own life, reflective of where you are at and what you are able to manage at the time. Your part in it is to accept it and work with it. If you fight the process, you are only fighting yourself. Surrender to what you experience and allow your process to unfold.

The more you heal and dissolve your layers, the more space you create within yourself for your jewel to shine.

Oh, and as for our dear Katherine who has journeyed in this process: the I Make a Difference process helped her to identify and to see clearly for the first time that she had actually stopped trusting herself. She had limited her choices, believing that she had no options. Her protective behaviors were detrimental in suppressing her well-being and eroding her self-belief and self-worth. With the tools she increased her awareness, such that there came a shift in her processing. She began to reconnect to herself and was open to new possibilities. She started to do right by herself, taking back her personal power, her choices.

Before moving to the next phase in the journey, let's review where you've travelled thus far.

THE I MAKE A DIFFERENCE ONION MODEL ADVENTURE

From chapter 4: The Creation of Your Layers
What facilitates your layers remaining in place:

- Personas
- Suppression
- Protection

From chapter 5: Preserving Your Layers
The conditioned behaviors, approaches, and processes that keep you protected and suppressed:

- Control
- Self-Talk
- What-Ifs
- Expectations
- Judgements
- Avoidance and Denial

From chapter 6: Inside Your Layers
The emotions requiring healing that are suppressed in your layers:

- Hatred
- Anger
- Hurt
- Guilt and Shame
- Rejection and Abandonment
- Loneliness
- Grief

From chapter 7: The Last Line of Protection
The underlying issues that lie at the bottom of each of your layers that protect you from connection to your jewel within:

- Neediness
- Vulnerability
- Self-Doubt
- Lack of Self-Belief
- Lack of Self-Worth

Your jewel within—the true you, and all the amazing qualities, aspects and elements of yourself, which as you unravel, heal, and dissolve your layers, you reconnect to, reclaim, and own:

- All the amazing qualities and attributes that make you who you are
- Your Knowing
- Your Truth
- Your Personal Power
- Your Light

- Your Internal Home
- The Real You
- You

All the elements of your onion require your attention, they require your time, they require you to develop your awareness, understanding, and ability to unravel the conditioning and heal the impacts. This is your adventure to bring you back to yourself, so you can be you. It requires you integrating all these different and separate parts of yourself.

The next chapter explores that integration process, the different phases involved, what they focus on, and how to work with each phase, so you can make even more of a difference to yourself, as you self-facilitate yourself to dissolve your layers and create the space for your jewel to shine and radiate light.

CHAPTER 8

INTEGRATION OF YOU

I find myself conversing with Alan, telling him what's going on with me and asking him a question. In response, he just sits there and says nothing. My self-talk is screaming at me, "He is not listening to me, he is ignoring me, he doesn't care!" I feel rejected, yet again. I am so needy to get some sort of response, so I know I am heard, so I know I am cared about, so I know I am important. What comes frothing from my mouth to him: "I am angry at you! You are not listening to me!"

Oh, how I know this pattern of interaction so well. The number of times I have experienced this situation over and over again. All the memories I can recall from my life when I have experienced this. And yet I have worked so consciously to change my reactions and how I approach this situation.

As I was accusing him, my words petered out midstream. Something was very different this time. Not different in the external experience; it was different in my internal processing. I didn't feel angry. I didn't feel any energy or physiological responses to the emotion and anger. I only had the words attached to the anger running through my head. The situation felt familiar and yet very very different. What was happening to me?

What was happening: I was experiencing evidence of my integration process. I had unraveled and healed the emotional and energy reactionary processing to this layer situation, and what remained was the mental processing.

There are three key phases to your integration process that you will experience in your travels to reclaiming the true you. This chapter explores the processes of these phases, so that you are able to recognize what you are experiencing and self-facilitate your processing with greater awareness.

THREE PHASES TO YOUR INTEGRATION

Integration is about you: retrieving, reclaiming, healing, and embracing the lost, separated, and fragmented parts of yourself so that you are whole again.

You may ask yourself, "Is this possible?"

Damn right it is! As you'll soon learn!

There are three key phases to this integration process:

1. Retrieving and reclaiming the memories stored in your subconscious mind.
2. Healing the mental, emotional, physical, energy, and spiritual impacts from your layers.
3. Being conscious of retrieving, reclaiming, and embracing your jewel, your amazing qualities, your knowing, your truth, and the real you.

You will experience all three of these integration phases simultaneously and individually as you journey towards being who you were born as and are. This chapter explores the processes of these three phases.

Your Integration Experience So Far

You may have already been experiencing the first phase of the integration process while you have been reading. Let me explain.

As you've been reading so far, have you noticed memories coming to your mind? They may be memories of experiences you have had recently or from your past? The memories may be uncomfortable or painful, or memories of happy times? Perhaps you have had stories and words running through your mind, felt emotions, and even physical sensations?

What you are experiencing is elements of your natural process of integration. As integration involves bringing together, merging, blending, and uniting things, and in this case—you. The memories you may have noticed coming back to you while you have been reading this book are an example of you retrieving and reclaiming the memories from your subconscious mind. This is phase one of the integration process. Any mental, emotional, or physical processing you experienced with the memories is an indicator of the areas for healing, which you'll learn about in phase two of the integration process.

Let's explore the three key phases in detail, starting with the first.

INTEGRATION PROCESS, PHASE 1

Retrieving and Reclaiming the Memories Stored in Your Subconscious Mind

How can you know what to unravel and heal if you don't remember the layer experiences?

Reclaiming the stored memories from your subconscious mind enables you to experience and know what you are to work with. This phase of the integration process is about retrieving and reclaiming.

The process of you storing memories stems right back to your first layer. In the ideal world, you are born fully conscious and aware, so when the first layer situation occurred where you were judged and rejected, you protected and suppressed aspects of yourself. You got hurt. Because you didn't and don't want to experience the situation or the pain again, you created a coping mechanism.

This coping mechanism involved a suppression of the memory. And the suppression process involves you storing the memory and the processing attached to the mental impacts of the situation in the back of your mind in your subconscious. You separated it from your conscious mind so that you didn't have to keep actively reliving the impacts of the hurt, the memory, and everything else that went with it.

Each time you put up a layer or added layers to your layers, you continued to store the entirety or part of your memories. Through doing this, you either fragmented or disconnected them from you. You conditioned this process of memory-storing out of a need to be safe and secure. Or so you believed.

The problem with this "safety mechanism" is that the suppressed memories lurk, waiting to weave their way back into your conscious mind. They find their way into your dreams, your daily processing, and your reactions. They are hidden, waiting to be triggered by a similar situation to the past original one. And when that similar situation does occur, what is triggered within you is the emotional and mental impacts and their conditioned processing from the layer experience—and they overwhelm and control you. You find yourself reacting to life rather than influencing it in a way that is right for you.

You can have buried the memory away so successfully in your subconscious mind that your denial gates have it imprisoned and in lockdown. If you have, then it may take some conscious work for each such buried memory to be retrieved. Or it will take healing of other layers and areas for the memory to be unlocked to reveal itself.

Suppressed memories will come to your conscious mind when you are ready to remember them. OR the memory may not be stored in your subconscious, and you relive it every day in your conscious mind.

A participant in one of the I Make a Difference programs, let's call him Tim, had fought in the Vietnam War. Tim shared that he could not sleep at night due to the dreams that he had. In his dreams he would relive the impacting war experiences over and over again. Staying awake enabled him to control the memory. The program resourced Tim with proactive ways to work with the memories and the processing that went with them during his waking state, so that he was able to sleep more easily again. So, whether your memories are suppressed or actively playing out, there are tools to process them out, unravel your conditioning, and find more peace within yourself.

Let me point out: it is not only your painful memories that you store in your subconscious mind. It is also the wonderful things you experienced in life that you could be suppressing.

Beautiful Memories

You likely have suppressed memories of the good and wonderful times as well. Why? There are several reasons: because you believe you don't deserve to have experienced them; and/or because the painful memories overrode and dominated the good times; and/or because the good memories bring up too much grief, as they highlight what you lost and don't have now.

Two questions to ask yourself: "Do I tend to remember more of the painful things that have happened to me or more of the wonderful things?" and "Why?"

The Wonderful and Painful Memories

Remembering only the good things or only the painful things can blur your reality and leave you suspended in elements of denial. In turn, this can have a huge impact on how you live your life.

If you only remember the good things, it can influence you in only seeing the wonderful things in your life. A beautiful place to be; however, it can end up un-beautiful. The "rose-colored glasses" you are wearing mean you don't see and acknowledge the things that require addressing, improving, or changing. Then the areas to be addressed can creep up on you and surprise and shock you out of denial at a time you least expect it.

Equally, if you only remember the painful things, then you may not see, receive, or accept the wonderful things in your life. Pessimism reigns, and the pity parties are great. So you (supposedly) "go without" in your life, seeing all that everyone else has and that you believe you haven't got. You are the one that is contributing to the life you are living.

A mix of the two—if you are someone who remembers both the wonderful and painful things in life, there will still be subtle and less obvious impacts on how you view things.

You may want to take time during your day to reflect on what you tend to focus on and what you tend to not see. This will give you insight into your memory process.

The integration process requires your subconsciously stored memories to come into your conscious mind, so you can remember them, see them, hear them, feel them, and work with them.

Where the memories are painful, they will come from the layer situations of your life. In order to heal the impacts of the layers, you need to be able to consciously recall the memory. Otherwise, how do you know what is influencing you or what you are to explore?

The memory entails mental processing, involving pictures and words. Once you recall it, it then triggers emotional, physical, energy, and spiritual processing. This moves you to phase two of the integration process.

To reclaim the beautiful things about yourself and your life, you need to be aware of them. You need to see and feel them so that you can reclaim and own them. Then you can build on your expression of them, your receiving them and experiencing them. Bringing those wonderful memories from your subconscious mind into your conscious mind is critical for you to reclaim yourself.

Identifying Reference Points

Reclaiming the wonderful memories provides you with reference points of the times when you were your true self. You separated from the amazing aspects of yourself when you rejected and abandoned the boy or girl you were at the first layer. As a result, finding your way back to that boy or girl requires you remembering. Recall in chapters 1 and 4, when I prompted you to remember when you felt safe, when you trusted yourself, and when you deserved the amazing things in life, even if it was only for a second, a minute, an hour, a day, or a period of time—the reason for this process was to assist you in connecting to your true self.

Having the reference points provides you with the evidence that who you truly are is real, possible and true.

In doing this, you are working with phase three of the integration process.

When memories come to your mind, it is an indicator that you are ready to work with them and the processing attached to them, so reassure yourself that this is part of your process. The memories would not have surfaced otherwise. Your system only gives you what you can handle. And, yes, in this way you are taking natural steps in reclaiming your trust in yourself, which is crucial in reclaiming your jewel within.

I remember being on a flight in the mid-2000s when suddenly out of the blue I had a memory of the beautiful, good, innocent, helpful, happy, and loving child I was at the age of four. I embodied the feelings, sensations, lightness, and freedom of energy and smiles. Wow, I cried at the recognition that I had been this wonderful child. I did have these qualities, and it was so beautiful to reconnect with this part of myself. No way was I not going to own these parts of myself. They were mine and they were me.

I have met people who have no memory recall before certain ages. The ages tend to be 7, 10, or 14 years old. If you experience this, make this OK as this can happen. In some cases, there may be experiences that were painful that you do not want to remember. You will remember them when you are meant to and ready to. If the memory is one that is overwhelming and you require support to work with it, ensure you seek help for doing so.

More often than not people's experience when they are unable to recall memories before a certain age is that the memories are actually the wonderful ones. They are not remembering them because the painful memories dominated and overwhelmed the good in their life. Trust that the beautiful memories will also come to you when you are meant to remember them so that you can embrace and own them. This is your natural process.

Self-Facilitation Activity—Integration Process, Phase 1—Retrieving and Reclaiming the Memories Stored in Your Subconscious Mind

In chapter 4, I recommended that you capture the memories from your past in your notebook or Personal Processing Workbook, as you would have an opportunity to explore them in chapter 8. With the memories that have come to mind and that you have captured spend some time free writing out your processing, utilizing the following information to prompt your processing.

Free write out, explore, and describe the memory:

a. Describe the situation you were in, detail what happened and who was involved.
b. Was the experience a layer situation or a beautiful experience?
c. What is the importance of this memory to you?

In describing the situation in detail you bring forward more of the memory from your subconscious mind. This enables you to see more broadly and clearly what happened so that some of the suppression and control over the memory are released. You then can identify the impacts of the experience and the processing you experience around the memory, which is what we explore in this next phase of integration.

INTEGRATION PROCESS, PHASE 2

Healing the Mental, Emotional, Physical, Energy, and Spiritual Impacts from Your Layers

You have reclaimed and retrieved a memory from a layer situation from your subconscious. Yes, phase one. And now you are experiencing the processing that goes with the memory. This is the second phase of the integration process.

Phase two kicks in, so if you are truly committed to reconnecting to the jewel within, it requires action. This phase is about healing the mental, emotional, physical, energy, and spiritual impacts from each of the layer situations. This is so you can dissolve the layers and operate from your jewel, your truth, and your knowing.

Each layer experience impacted you in either all or some of the following ways: mentally, emotionally, physically, energy-wise, and spiritually. To heal and dissolve your layers, it requires you to be aware of and understand how your processing functions at each of these levels.

Mental Impacts

Your mental processing comes in the form of memories, pictures, and words. They are wrapt up in your beliefs, self-talk, what-ifs, judgements, and expectations (remember, these are the conditioned behaviors that keep elements of you suppressed and protected as described in chapter 5, Preserving Your Layers).

Working with your mental processing requires identifying where the conditioned responses—the words, questions, stories, beliefs, and chatter—originated from. Then downloading the words, through verbalizing or writing them out, to ensure you get them out of you so you can work with changing the pattern of the conditioning. This assists in healing and diminishing the power the mental impacts have had on you.

Let's return to the situation I described at the opening of the chapter where I'm talking to my partner Alan, but he's not responding to me in the way I wanted him to, so my self-talk is screaming, "He is not listening to me!" As I wrote, I identified that the mental processing was all that was remaining from the layer situation. It required me to explore my beliefs and change the pattern of the words.

The beliefs I identified from the layer situation related to men not listening to me because I believed that what I felt was of no interest to them. I explored the evidence of the reality of this belief to discover that this was now not the case with Alan. Alan was listening; however, he did not need to provide a response as he knew I was capable of managing my own processing. So I worked with the girl in me from the original layer situation reinforcing that we (the girl and I) had experienced this type of situation in the past and that now we were having new experiences, ones where men—Alan—do listen and do care about what we feel and that we had the evidence that this was the case.

You will have an opportunity to explore the process of working with your beliefs in chapter 9.

Your mental process has the stories and conversations that require unravelling of conditioning, the memories for healing and reclaiming, and the limiting beliefs for releasing, so they can be replaced by new helpful ones. Your mental process gives words and pictures to your emotional, sensory, energy, physical and spiritual processes.

Emotional Impacts

You will feel your emotional processing in the functioning of your body. You will experience in your body physiological processes including sensations, breathing and heartbeat changes, and temperature and energy fluctuations. These are examples of how your physical system reacts to and expresses the effects of the emotions you are experiencing.

The emotional impacts from your past leak out of the layers or come gushing at you in physical ways. If you received support as a child to process out your emotions at the time the layer situation occurred, rather than suppress them, then you would not have suppressed your emotions and you would have no emotional impacts.

You will be familiar with what you experience internally when you feel emotions. What is important is to identify what exactly the emotion is that you are feeling and then process and work with healing it.

To return to the scenario I described at the start of the chapter: the emotion that was previously triggered when I felt I was not heard, that would race through my body, was anger. When the layer situation was triggered, I would have a raging bull in my belly full of fire, energy, and power, my heartbeat would increase, and my chest would want to explode.

As I said, I worked consciously to change this reaction, as it would be expressed externally, impact others, and create outcomes I was not happy about. And I was responsible for those undesirable outcomes, so healing the impacts required working with the girl inside myself from the original layer, the girl that felt such pain, anger, and rejection. Integration entailed me accepting the emotions and allowing this girl inside myself to express what she felt, knowing it was safe to do so.

Physical Impacts

Your physical processing is about what you experience with your body whereas the physiological processing is the body's response to the emotions. An example of this is the effect of an injury, like a broken bone: the physical element is the break of the bone while a physiological effect of that broken bone is the body's response to it, such as shock and pain. If someone purposely hurt you that resulted in you breaking your bone, then you will also experience emotions like hurt, anger, and rejection, to name a few. The physiological response to the emotion could be tears, heat, sweating, rapid heart beat, and tightness in the chest. Physical impacts from layers will have emotional, mental, and energy impacts as well.

The physical impacts from the layers can be glaringly obvious, similar to the impact of an accident: broken bones, loss of a limb, loss of hearing or sight, being sick, physical violence, the impacts of anorexia or bulimia, or where you have scars from beatings.

The physical impacts can be very subtle as well and can take a reasonable amount of awareness to identify. Take, for example, as a child, someone yelled at you. At the time you hunched your shoulders up, tensed your face, and shut yourself down internally. This was to protect yourself.

From that day on every time you hear someone using a tone that is similar to the original situation, you will potentially react in the same physical manner. You will hunch your shoulders, tense your face, and shut down internally. You may not even be aware this is happening. This is you feeling vulnerability and directing the emotion and energy into your body, which can create issues with your shoulders, back, and neck.

By developing your awareness of this, you can work with your physical reaction to unwind it and change it. That way, when a triggering situation happens again, the moment you physically react, you can consciously choose to relax your shoulders, let go of the tension in your face, and focus on relaxing your body. In this relaxed state you can work more effectively with your mental and emotional processing as you are not controlling them and trying to shut them down.

This integration process assists you to work with healing the physical impacts from the layers, where physically possible.

During an I Make a Difference session I was facilitating, David shared his story of how he had been placed in a boy's home when he was young. There he would be strapped into a jacket, which would restrict his movement so that the people could inflict pain upon him with the aim of changing his behaviors. As David was exploring the emotions he experienced from this past situation, he actually physically felt the pain and restriction of the jacket digging into his back. David's body held the memory of it. The awareness he gained of what he was experiencing physically provided him with the direction for the healing and unravelling of the conditioning from this layer.

Energy Impacts

You feel drained, squeezed, backstabbed, suffocated, drawn off, fragmented, bled dry, burdened, blocked, and beaten up. And all you did was go shopping at the supermarket, have coffee with friends, or go to work for the day. Oh, the energy impacts attached to all the other processing you experience from the layers.

You have your life-force energy and your physical energy. Your physical energy is impacted by how you treat yourself physically, in relation to diet, exercise, sleep, and the amount of physical activity or non-activity you engage in. There are many books and sources available to guide and support you in managing this type of energy.

The focus here is on your life-force energy, which is the natural flow of energy you feel and experience through your being. This energy is influenced by and attached to your emotions, thoughts, and especially your intentions. Any thinking or feeling process has energy circling within it; you can feel it.

Your life-force energy is impacted by other people, and you impact others and yourself through the processing and expression of your control, expectations, judgements, avoidance, denial, emotions, guilt, rejection, vulnerability, and neediness, i.e., all the elements contained within your layers.

When you suppress anything internally and protect yourself, you are personally impacting your own energy. You knot the energy up, create a block, and prevent it from flowing freely, as you are controlling what you are experiencing.

Remember the times you have felt a knot in your stomach, tightness in your chest or throat? These are examples of you controlling your emotions and preventing them from surfacing. You are blocking the free flow of what is naturally happening within.

Emotional neediness, created by the "lack of" in your life, will drive you to give and give and give away your energy to the people you are emotionally needy of. Or you take on board others' issues and the responsibility and energy attached to their issues. Either way, you draw people into your life that are needy of you and you are needy of them, and you drain yourself by giving to them and rescuing them.

Each time you take responsibility for other people's issues, emotional processing, and learnings you take on board energy that is a burden and obligation. That is self-imposed.

Through walking beside people supporting them to take responsibility for their own process, rather than you rescuing, saving, or protecting them, you release this energy drain from yourself.

Your energy is also impacted significantly by others' judgements, expectations, and rejection. If a person is judging or rejecting you, then they are projecting their emotional issues onto you. The energy attached to the emotions is thrown or directed at you. You can feel this it is like knives in your back or a slap in the face. If they have expectations of you, then you will feel the pressure and weight of the energy. However, you can only truly be impacted by another person's energy if you have some emotional attachment to the person or situation, or their judgement and rejection buys into yours of yourself. You will also experience this when you have expectations, judgements, or rejection of yourself.

Anytime someone is angry, hurt, or upset with you and they direct it at you, they will send energy in your direction. Energy you do not deserve. A group of young people in Port Augusta, Australia, termed it as "directed." This meant you were directing your energy and issues at someone (or vice versa). And this has impacts.

When you suppress emotional and mental processing, given that emotions and thoughts are filled with energy, the suppression creates a block in your internal life force and energy flow. You can get stressed and tired. If the energy is not expressed, then it needs to go somewhere and can contribute to impacting your physical state.

When I have experienced feeling useless, the first indicator that something was happening for me was the block of energy that tightened within my body. I also felt like I could not move forward in any direction. It was like I had been put in concrete and was stuck in one spot. The control and suppression of the feeling and thoughts of being useless were expressed in energy that was impacting my being.

The more you express and heal your mental, emotional, and physical processing in a healthy way, the more energy you will have because it will flow freely within you. You are not controlling or blocking your natural process. You are working with it and managing it.

Your energy is for one person and one person only—you.

This is about giving back to people their own energy and issues, reclaiming your energy and issues from others, and working to stop trying to control and fight your own process.

Working with healing, the energy impacts of the layers enables you to connect to the strong, energy-filled life force you have at your core.

Spiritual Impacts

There are lots of different interpretations of spirituality and you will have your own connection to what spirituality is or is not, so I will not provide a definition of it. It can be your connection to your jewel and your godliness. Your connection to the universe. Or your connection to religion. Your connection to spirit. Or your connection to your cultural ancestry and beliefs.

The layer experiences can have impacted you spiritually and your spiritual process.

I remember a person saying, "God abandoned me as a child." They actually felt this had happened. They believed that if God had been with them, then God would not have allowed the painful things they had experienced to have happened to them.

There are people I have met who remember seeing and talking with spirit when they were a child. The other people in their life did not understand them, and in some cases they were judged for what they experienced. The impact was that they shut this side of themselves down. They suppressed and separated from their connection with spirit.

Through the integration process, they have reclaimed this connection.

For some indigenous cultures I have had the honor of sharing with, their spirituality is the connection to the earth, their ancestors, and the stars.

Whatever spirituality means to you, this part of the process is about healing any impacts the layer experiences have had on your connection to your spirituality.

The Overall Healing Process

As you consciously work on healing these areas impacted by the layer experiences, some areas will heal faster than others. There is no set series of steps to it. It is your unique process that will unfold at the time and rate it is meant to take. Be aware that the process may be different for each layer. Let's look at some scenarios for how the healing process can unfold.

Say, you have retrieved a memory from your subconscious mind that is connected to a layer. You have worked with healing the impacts from that layer. Then you find a situation arises again, similar to this previous layer situation. The memory is immediately in your mind, and the impacts are triggered.

This time, though, what is different is that you don't feel anything emotionally or energy-wise. What you still have is residue mental processing with the words going through your head. This is what happened to me in the situation I described in the chapter's opening where I was needy to be heard by my partner Alan. And when my layer attached to this situation was triggered, I discovered I wasn't angry anymore; the only impact I experienced was at a mental level. It was residue conditioning of the mental processing attached to the situation. In the moment I was able to acknowledge this as well as the growth I had done in terms of what I was no longer experiencing internally. I also recognized that I was imposing my past experiences on Alan and that he was not the issue.

In being aware of your processing, you will recognize you potentially have healed the emotions and energy from the situation. And there still remains some healing with the mental process. Be aware of which process and impact you are working with at the time, and recognize the progress you have made.

Often you will find that you will heal the emotional, mental, and energy impacts, and the final healing is expressed through the body in some form.

Or you heal the physical impacts, and then the emotions come to the surface.

For six months I had a few lesions appear on my lower legs and lower arms. I went through all the medical tests, and there was nothing to indicate why this was happening. The suggestion was for me to change the soap I used. I did this; however, the lesions did not heal.

Through my acceptance and love of my body for being so awesome through healing all the other impacts, one day the lesions started vanishing. The previous two years I underwent a cathartic process of healing the remaining significant emotional, mental, and energy impacts from my past. My body was the last area for releasing what I had experienced. I see these lesions as a final physical release, and my body's healing of them as a healing of the final area of impact.

When you view your healing and growth with the natural curiosity you have, the discovery of what is different and how you have healed, as well as how you have changed and what you can do to continue to develop, you'll find it a fascinating adventure.

Self-Facilitation Activity—Integration Process, Phase 2—Healing the Mental, Emotional, Physical, Energy, and Spiritual Impacts from Your Layers

In the self-facilitation activity integration process phase 1 of this chapter, you explored the memories that have come to your mind since reading this book. For any of those memories that are attached to layer experiences, you now have an opportunity with this activity to identify and explore the impacts of those situations on you.

For each of the memories you explored identify:

a. The mental impacts: this includes the stories, words, judgements, expectations, and any pictures that stand out in your mind.

b. The emotional impacts: the emotions you experienced and any physiological reactions you experience.

c. The physical impacts: what you experienced in your body that you still experience today.

d. The energy impacts: how your life force has been impacted, including any draining, blocks, or heaviness.

e. The spiritual impacts: how your connection to what you deem spiritual was affected by what happened.

INTEGRATION PROCESS, PHASE 3

Being Conscious of Retrieving, Reclaiming, and Embracing Your Jewel, Your Amazing Qualities and Attributes, Your Knowing, Your Truth, and the Real You

At this point your attention is potentially absorbed in working with your layer memories and the processing that goes with it. Even still, ensure you keep a watchful eye out for the parts of yourself that start to surface that are you, the true you.

As you heal and dissolve your layers, the elements and aspects that are natural to the true you will make more of their presence felt as they shine through.

This phase of your integration is about you growing your ability to become fully conscious of your knowing, your truth, and your jewel; growing your ability to consciously reclaim and embrace your amazing qualities and attributes. This is so you can own them and express them, so they are you.

At the first layer, you rejected and abandoned the boy or girl you were, some of your amazing qualities, your jewel, your truth, you, and your self-trust. You became separated from these parts of yourself, and they became fragmented.

Phase one of the integration process involves you retrieving the wonderful memories from your subconscious mind. This is so you reclaim the qualities you felt and expressed during that memory and own them. In doing so, you are able to retrieve your connection to your knowing and truth, which is where all the answers are that you require for yourself. In listening to your knowing and truth and acting on them, you trust yourself. You respect yourself. You love yourself. You are reclaiming who you truly are.

The memories you have of times when you were the natural and real you provide you with tangible connections to the parts of yourself you separated from. Then you can reclaim them so that you can integrate them into who you are today. To be who you were born as and are, and be conscious of your knowing, your truth, and your amazing qualities requires you to see them, feel them, know them, own them, trust them, express them, and share them.

This is you giving yourself permission to be you, and then your jewel shines within and out of you.

Self-Facilitation Activity—Integration Process, Phase 3—Being Conscious of Retrieving, Reclaiming, and Embracing Your Jewel, Your Amazing Qualities and Attributes, Your Knowing, Your Truth and the Real You

With the memories that have come to mind that you captured in the first self-facilitation activity in this chapter, this activity is a chance for you to explore the beautiful and wonderful memories. If there are other memories like these that have arisen but you've not yet captured them, include these as well. Spend time free writing out your processing, utilizing the following information to prompt you:

Free write out, explore, and describe the memory.

   a. Describe the situation you were in, detail what happened and who was involved.
   b. What is the importance of this memory?
   c. What did you feel, what were you like, what were the amazing things about you that you remember in this memory?

Bringing these memories forward to your conscious mind provides you with the opportunity to reinforce the reference point we explored earlier in the chapter. A reference point of the true you and the amazing qualities that make you who you are. Through being conscious of how your amazing qualities and attributes, your jewel, your knowing, your truth, and the real you are expressed mentally as well as how they feel energy-wise and physically, you are able to tangibly know and identify them. That way, you can own them and integrate them into who you are today.

The Integration Process

All the natural phases of your integration process are in play, as you work through each of the chapters in this book. Acceptance of what you experience is the key to you being able to facilitate yourself through the phases. Make everything you think, feel, and process OK. You are experiencing what you are experiencing because you are ready to explore each element. And you are ready to unravel and dissolve your layers to heal and excitingly reclaim the wonderful parts of yourself that are surfacing.

The situation I experienced that I shared at the beginning of this chapter, where I projected my issues onto Alan became such a gift for me to gain insight into my integration process. I mentioned that the words petered out as I was sharing how angry I was. What happened is that I paused and checked in with myself on what was going on for me. Then I was able to share with clarity the truth of my processing. The words I said were, "I am angry. However, I am not really, I just have the words in my head, which are lingering from a past situation, as I used to be angry in situations where I believed I was not being listened to." My partner looked at me with curiosity and shared that he had heard every word I said, and the reason he did not respond straight away was that he was processing his own response to what I'd said.

There you go, a new outcome and a new experience for me, both internally and externally.

So, through taking time to connect to my processing I was able to identify the difference I was experiencing and own the healing I have done. This supported me to express the truth of what was happening for me, as opposed to repeating a conditioned pattern of expression. In turn Alan was able to share his processing and I heard it. Instead of a fight, we connected in our understanding of each other. This is the beauty of integration and embarking on the I Make a Difference adventure.

I knew there were still steps I needed to take to heal and change the conditioning of the residue mental processing to fully dissolve the layer. This required me working with the beliefs and the patterns of the words that I was conditioned with.

Your beliefs are a significant part of your mental processing. They hugely impact whether you keep repeating the layer situations over and over and over again—or not. They influence your approach and ability to work with all the elements of your onion and the phases of integration.

You have a sensational opportunity in the next chapter to explore some of your beliefs, gain insight into the influence of your beliefs, and develop your ability to change or let go of any of your beliefs so that you have new experiences in your life.

CHAPTER 9

BELIEFS WITHIN THE LAYERS

"You want to create a documentary on my journey and work—why?" I ask.

Ben, the workshop participant, responds, "It is for a project for film school. I want to call it 'From Pain to Profit'."

What flies out of my mouth in response: "We are not in business to make a profit."

What the ???!!!!! I hear what I just said, and I am flabbergasted. "What on earth are we in business to do then?" I ask myself, as I become needy to understand and stop the feelings of anxiety that are brewing.

The answer I get: "To help people do the right thing and to be good people in what we do." This feels right. However, I notice I have some conflict starting to surface in my belly.

The next belief that weaves its way up from the depths of my subconscious mind and reveals itself to me: "We are in business to cover expenses."

This explained so much. Here was the answer as to why my business was just getting through and breaking even financially. This belief that had just shot from my mouth was conditioned mental processing, straight-from-my-unconscious reaction to the word "profit." I'd been totally unaware of what I'd said—and the belief behind it—until I heard the words I spoke. This is how a belief I had buried in my subconscious mind chose at that moment to become transparent.

Oh wow, how this belief had been driving my behaviors, my decision-making, and my approach to business. I needed to get to the bottom of it and find out more about the belief if I was going to experience something different. So the next question I asked myself was "What is wrong with making a profit?"

The answer I get shocked me, floored me, and left me feeling really mixed up about money and being a good person. My answer: "Only bad people make a profit." OMG, where on earth did this belief come from? I not only had layers; now I also had belief layers in the layers. I had to find the origins of this belief, so I went searching.

As I was growing up, there were wealthy people my family was associated with. What they did and how they behaved, in my world and to me, was bad. It wasn't right, and what I sensed off them felt wrong.

This is where the belief I had been carrying around since childhood stemmed from. I had interpreted what I experienced into "If you made a profit and had money, you were a bad person." And this, of course, conflicted with my beliefs about growing, developing, and becoming the true you, a process about being a good person. Wow, what a revelation! Wow, how many years it has impacted me! Umm, now what to do about this belief?

Your beliefs are incorporated into your memories and mental processing. They underpin and lie within the expression of your judgements, self-talk, what-ifs, and expectations. In chapter 4, The Creation of Your Layers, you explored where the boy or girl in yourself from the layer either took on board other people's words and stories, or you created your own to fill in the gap and explain what you were experiencing. This is the process with beliefs. And they have a significant influence on all of the behaviors, approaches, processes, emotions, and underlying issues from your layers.

Your ability to facilitate your healing—dissolve and cease the repeated pattern of occurrence of the situations from the layers—is at the mercy of whether you believe you can. This chapter provides you with the opportunity to not only explore your beliefs but also to delve into how they influence you. That way you can work with them to support your journey in reconnecting to yourself.

Behaviors, Attitude, Values, and Beliefs, and How They Influence Each Other

How your onion was created, as you are aware, has its origins in the past. And as you have explored, your past does not make you who you are; however, it does condition and impact you, providing you with insight into what is right and not right for yourself. Yes, it has an influence on you and can have a limiting hold on you, even now. However, it was not just you and the people in your home environment that influenced the conditioning and impacts; others were involved as well.

Just about everyone and everything you have been exposed to and interacted with has had a level of influence on you. This includes family, friends, school, history, government, teachers, religion, books, the internet, and movies. As well as Facebook, culture, bosses, and work colleagues, to name a few.

The people and factors not only left impressions on the areas of your life from the onion model; they also had an effect on your behaviors, attitudes, values, and beliefs. These are additional areas for you to be aware of as you facilitate your growth and development.

All of these areas are interconnected in how they impact each other. They also relate to each of the areas on the onion model and the phases of integration.

An important first step is recognizing which aspects of your behaviors, attitudes, values, and beliefs are visible and tangible because they are the external expression of what you experience internally. Also recognizing which aspects are an internal process. You don't see them, but you may make assumptions about them, based on the behavior and your external experience.

Are behaviors, attitudes, values, and beliefs something you can see or not see? Whether you can see them has an influence on your identification of the process you are working with.

Outside of You

- *Behaviors*—you can see them; the external expression of the elements on the onion model: the behaviors, approaches, processes, emotions, underlying issues, amazing qualities, your self-belief, and self-worth; physical and verbal processing

Inside of You

- *Attitudes*—you can't see them, but you can feel and sense them; the internal expression of your outlook, how you see things, how you feel about things emotionally and physically, and the energy you put out in terms of intentions and emotions; mental, emotional, energy, physiological, and spiritual processing
- *Values*—you can't see them; mental, emotional, energy, and spiritual processing
- *Beliefs*—you can't see them; mental, emotional, energy, and spiritual processing

In the chapter's "pain to profit" opening example, these were my subconscious beliefs: "Only bad people make a profit," "We are in business to help people, do the right thing, and be good people in what we do," and "We are in business to cover expenses."

These are the values attached to these beliefs: truth, integrity, people, and doing the right thing.

The attitude, emotions, and outlook immersed in this situation involved me emotionally rejecting money, making a profit, and bad people. I was needy of doing the right thing and that I did not put others out of pocket. Also, I felt guilty and responsible for ensuring that I make the cost of the program and services at a rate that others could afford. All of these elements influenced the decision-making in the business.

This resulted in behaviors where I would let people attend the course at a lower rate than what I charged. And in some cases for free. Consequently, the investment cost to attend the program and services enabled us to only just cover expenses.

The impact of this unconscious limiting belief on the business meant that the I Make a Difference program was marketed on a shoestring and required lots of hard and time-consuming leg work. As the income earned from the program did not reflect the time, quality, and worth my colleague and I brought to it. My what-if: if only I had uncovered this belief hidden within myself and worked to release it sooner, then the public I Make a Difference program would have had a different journey reaching more people with financial abundance to support it.

Key point: growing your awareness of what you are doing externally and experiencing internally will support you to identify the aspects of yourself that you want to work with so that you can make a difference in your processing and life.

It's amazing the processing that goes on inside of you and the impacts it has on your outside world!

External Expression

Your external expression is the most obvious, tangible aspect of yourself that you can be aware of. Your *behaviors* are what you express to the outside world. They are visible and audible in what you do and say. And what influences how you behave is what you are processing internally. Internally your attitude, beliefs, and values drive your external expression.

You can observe a person behaving in a certain way, and immediately you interpret what they are doing and why they are doing it. You make an assumption and a judgement about their behavior. And you make up stories as to what their internal values, attitudes, and beliefs are that are driving their behavior.

Your interpretation of what they are doing is based on YOUR past experiences. And your past experiences will be different from the other person's.

No two people ever have the same experience. They might appear the same; however, each person will perceive it, interpret it, and behave differently with regards to the experience because their pasts and the influences from the past are different.

This was in my face during one of our programs. Josh, a young participant, had been brilliant all week in his attention, contributions, and approach to the sessions. However, suddenly he changed on the last day. Josh started swearing, judging the program and the facilitator, disrupting others, and behaving very differently from how he had. Ahhh, I had enough and was about to react and have a go at him. Then I became aware of what I was about to do. I recognized at that moment that I was reacting to one of my past situations. A situation where I had experienced people behaving in the same manner and rejecting the program and me. This is where my belief of Josh's behavior came from.

So, I changed my approach and sat and talked with Josh to understand him. I began, "I just want to check in with you. Are you OK, as you seem different to how you have been in the last week, and I want to know if I can support you in any way?"

Josh paused, breathed, tears started welling up, and the truth came out. This young man was struggling emotionally because his best friend had been hit by a train the night before. My initial interpretation of his behavior had been based on my past experiences and not on what was truly happening for him.

The most powerful thing to do at the time you observe a behavior or hear words where you make an assumption about them is to pause and ask questions: "Why did you say that?" "Why did you do that?" Understand the other person's processing and where they are coming from.

What you are doing is checking out if the picture in your head is the same as theirs. If it's not, then you can tune into their process.

Also, you can apply this same process to yourself. There are times when you may not be aware of why you say things or behave in certain ways. The moment you are aware that this is the case, ask yourself similar questions to what you would ask others, so you can explore your attitude, values, and beliefs that are driving your external expression. Your self-awareness then enables you to not only understand yourself more; it also enables you to decide whether you want to change or develop what you have discovered.

Asking questions, both of others and of yourself, builds understanding.

Internal Processing

Your internal processing involves your attitude, values, and beliefs.

Your *attitude* is about how you are feeling at any point in time, how you see things, and your outlook. Your attitude is expressed in words in the thoughts that run through your head.

Your attitude is strongly influenced by your intentions, emotional state, and physical state. Others cannot tangibly see or hear your attitude until you express some behavior externally. What they can do though is feel and sense your attitude. Your intentions and emotions emit energy, and this is what others can pick up from you.

If someone says to you, "You have a bad attitude," they are not taking responsibility for describing the behavior you are demonstrating that signals to them you have a bad attitude. They are making an assumption, and that assumption is based on their past.

Ask them, "What is it I am doing or saying that tells you that?" This will support the person to be accountable for their comment and will provide you with the information as to what they are seeing.

In my situation with Josh who was upset, I made the assumption that his attitude towards the program was one of rejection. That he did not want to be there and that he had had enough of what we were covering. How wrong I was! Yes, Josh was feeling rejection, but it was his own self-rejection that he had not been there to help his friend. So I was sensing the right emotion; however, I was interpreting it in my way, not his way.

Your values and beliefs will be expressed in your attitude, and they also strongly influence your behavior. Your beliefs and values are not visible, and you cannot see them until a behavior is demonstrated that expresses them.

Your *values* are what is important to you right now. They are your preferences and priorities and what is most dear and precious to you. They strongly influence your decision-making.

You will have values that are consistently the same throughout your whole life, as they are your principles that make your foundation. Examples of these are freedom, trust, truth, and/or family.

A person I had a relationship with wanted to pay for everything for me. One of my core values is freedom, so you can imagine my reaction to him. I felt like I was being owned. The relationship did not last long. And the beliefs that were attached to my value of freedom were limiting me, especially in receiving in relationships. It took me a few years to discover and unravel these. I also discovered that my lack of self-worth contributed to my decision-making in this situation.

Some of your values will change during your life, dependent on what stage of life you are experiencing. As a child, you may have valued fun and friends. As a teenager, it may have been freedom and entertainment. As a young adult, it may be employment, studying, or saving. As a parent, it may be providing and safety. And later on in life, it might be family, independence, and/or travel.

Then there will be values that can change during the day, dependent on the situation you are in and where your focus is. If you are at work, your values may be safety, customers first, or adding value. Then when you get home, your values may be family and relaxation.

Values have a significant influence and role to play when you experience conflict within yourself where you go against what is right and true for yourself. Such as when you don't want to do something and yet you go and do it. Also when there is disagreement, tension, argument, or some form of conflict with other people.

An example of this is where you come home from work, and your partner wants to talk to you and share what they have been doing during the day. However, you want to relax and have some downtime. Two different values are operating at this point, so there is tension between the two of you. The reason the emotions surface is because of the neediness you both have to be important and valued. You both want what is important for your individual self to take prominence: the values of sharing and understanding versus the values of relaxation and time out.

What do you do? Both of you battle it out and get annoyed with each other until one of you resentfully gives in. Why is it both of you can't just share what is important to each of you and then work out how both of you can have your values respected? Oh, that requires understanding, communication and cooperation? Uh-huh, outmoded processes.

Please don't view it as "to compromise." Why?

Ponder on a time when you have compromised. Actually go down and feel the process. What did it feel like for you?

More often than not, when you compromise, you give something up. You lose something or miss out on something. Why? That's right—to keep the peace, and it is easier. When you stop and truly ponder on it, if you are compromising, then you are operating from a lack of self-worth. You are not important enough and you do not deserve to have your value and what you want honored and respected.

If you are happy to go with something because you are accepting and you are not giving up something that is important to you, then this is a different process to compromise. It may look the same on the outside, but the intention and the processing internally are different.

It is still OK to compromise if you are happy to do so. However, take responsibility for any feelings that surface later where you feel you have lost or given something up.

If you are not fully aware of your values and you want to be, spend some time answering the following questions:

- What are the core things that are important to me?
- What lies behind what I will stand strong on that is important to me?

Values tend to be one or two words, like "truth," "family," or "customers first." Beliefs are the sentences and explanations of something, including the reasoning for your values.

Your *beliefs* are what you believe to be true or not true at this current point in time. They are your truth, opinions, and views. They underpin all of your conscious and unconscious processing.

The more conscious and aware you are of your beliefs, the more you will be able to identify why you do what you do, think what you do, say what you do, and feel how you do. The more you understand your own beliefs, the more you will see that other people's beliefs may be similar to yours, extremely different, or somewhere else on the spectrum between these extremes.

What is imperative with beliefs is never assume what another person believes. Never assume what is driving their behaviors. Ask them questions, instead, such as "Why did you do that?," "Why did you say that?" This will enable you to check if your processing is aligned with them or not.

The next section of this chapter is totally dedicated to beliefs and more importantly, your beliefs. Beliefs are the prominent process with regards to what you experience and whether you can work with your past layers and discover your jewel.

Beliefs

Beliefs are a mental process that has a significant impact on your emotional state and the outcomes that happen in your life. They influence the choices you make, how you interpret things, your communication, interactions, what you see, what you hear, and how you react or respond.

Your beliefs are expressed in your self-talk, what-ifs, judgements, expectations, and all of your emotions and underlying issues. As we have discussed, beliefs are what we believe to be true or not true, right now. Beliefs can change in a second, dependent on your experience and further information you learn or find out. They generally take the form of a sentence: "Boysenberry ice cream is the best" or "Men should be the providers."

Your beliefs can be limiting for you. They can prevent you from healing your emotions and dissolving your layers. In fact, they can influence you so that you keep experiencing recurring patterns of situations and outcomes over and over again reinforcing your layers.

Or they can be helpful and supportive in your unravelling, healing, growth, and development. They can assist you to change the pattern of your past experiences, experience new outcomes, grow your self-belief and self-worth, and be more true to who you truly are.

You have subconscious and conscious beliefs that are conditioned from what you have been told by other people, groups of people, organizations, cultures, and society in general. Many of your beliefs you will believe to be true, but there are often some beliefs you have that actually aren't yours and yet they influence you on a daily basis.

An example of this is "Men should not cry." Says who? Where did this come from and do you truly believe this? "Big girls don't cry." Says who? Where did this one come from? And yet it is so widely believed and/or expressed in society.

Damn it, as a human you can cry if you want or need to! You have tear ducts, and they were made for expressing tears, so if you want to cry, cry, and if you don't, don't.

You have two different layers to your beliefs. The conscious layer and the unconscious layer.

Conscious beliefs—these are your beliefs that you are aware of, you voice them and know them. You might believe that chicken is nicer than pork or that a particular sports team is the best.

Unconscious beliefs—these are beliefs that you are not aware of. This is where you do not know why you do or say the things you do or say. They are beliefs that are hidden within your subconscious mind, driving your thoughts, emotions, and actions. You do not know they are there, and they are often at a deeper layer of processing.

Your unconscious beliefs are the most powerful ones in their influence over you. You generally know if you have discovered an unconscious belief when you feel uncomfortable about the belief or where you get a thud in the stomach. The more you can bring these beliefs from your subconscious mind to your conscious mind, the more influence you have over them, your choices, and the outcomes you experience.

Beliefs are part of your integration process that we explored in chapter 8. They are an element of the mental processing attached to the memories for retrieval that you stored in your subconscious mind, and you will uncover unconscious beliefs in this process.

Unconscious beliefs will influence some of the patterns of the layer situations that keep recurring in your life. For you to be able to change these patterns, they will either require you to go looking for them or be very aware of when they do come to your mind.

They will be expressed in what you say and do, and they require you to hear and see them and ask yourself, "Why did I say that?" or "Why do I believe that?" or "Why did I do that?" This will enable you to make your unconscious beliefs conscious so that you can work with them. You can own and grow them because they are helpful to you and your life. Or you can change them because they may be limiting you.

How Beliefs Influence You

Your beliefs have power to either limit or support you in unravelling, healing, dissolving, growing, and developing yourself.

They influence everything about you. Your behaviors, your decision-making, what you think, and what you see and hear. As well as how you see and feel about yourself and others, what you say, your relationships, and the outcomes you experience.

You will look for evidence to reinforce your beliefs, so as to justify your actions and thoughts to yourself. To prove your beliefs are right.

For example: if you believe a person is unfair in their approach, then what you look for and find in them is everything that they do and say that is unfair. This reinforces your belief.

Your beliefs will either limit or support you in your growth and in life through reinforcing layers, or they help you to heal and change your layers.

For example: I had a belief that all men are going to leave me. This belief kept reinforcing one of my layers as I kept experiencing being left. The behaviors I demonstrated in response to the belief, I was not even conscious of. I did things that pushed men away, thus contributing to them leaving, or I sat waiting for them to leave and never got truly close.

Your beliefs influence the outcomes you experience. They become self-fulfilling prophecies. What you believe becomes what you experience.

For example: if you believe you are a bad speller, what are you going to be? A bad speller. You won't be open to learning and developing your spelling. If you believe that healing yourself is going to take a long time, then it will take a long time. And potentially you will subconsciously do things to prolong it.

You are likely to be drawn to people who support and reinforce your beliefs. You feel safe and secure with these people as they reassure you and your belief. And you do not have to face the fact that your belief may not be fully true.

You may fight, resist, or try and sway people with different beliefs.

Why would you want to try to fight, resist, or try and persuade people with different beliefs? You would only do this if you do not fully believe in your own belief.

Or you are accepting of other people's beliefs because you believe in your own beliefs and are accepting of them.

You can have one experience, take on or create a belief, and impose it on all other experiences.

For example: I had a belief that all men who drank a lot were violent. I would go to the pub. If a guy asked if I wanted a drink, I would think, "They are out to have a go at me," so I would react. When I stepped back and asked myself, "How many men in my life that drank a lot were also violent?" The answer: only two. But I labelled every man that I'd ever met with this belief.

Self-Facilitation Activity—Your Beliefs

Now you have a chance to explore your beliefs. So grab your pen and notebook (or Personal Processing Workbook). The objective of this activity is to support you to identify some of the beliefs you have about particular areas of your life. This activity will provide you with an opportunity to explore your conscious and unconscious beliefs. You can then let go of any that are limiting and own and strengthen the beliefs that are helpful.

There are five stages to this process of exploring your beliefs that you will work through, and they include:

1. Write down your beliefs.
2. Identify—*helpful* or *limiting*.
3. Determine—*true* or *not true*.
4. Transform any limiting beliefs to helpful beliefs.
5. Act on helpful beliefs.

This process will enable you to work with your beliefs whenever you choose to.

In your notebook or Personal Processing Workbook, take some time to do some free writing and explore the following:

Step One: Write Down Your Beliefs

Identify and capture on paper the beliefs you have on each of the following topics. I have provided a question for you to pose to yourself next to each topic if you need some prompting. Write down the first responses you get, don't question them as they are the beginning of your processing for this topic. Your answers will tend to be a sentence.

If you get stuck at all—say, your mind goes blank—then think of something completely different, such as the beach or a nice dinner, and then come back and ask yourself the question again. Taking your mind off something, then coming back to it, allows your process to free up for the information to come to you.

If you are interested in exploring any unconscious beliefs, it is a matter of writing all your answers down and then exploring the questions further. You may even ask yourself after you have written some of your responses, "Why do I believe that?" Keep writing, capturing the layers of belief you get until there are no more answers. See what you unravel and uncover.

An indicator that you have uncovered an unconscious belief is when you feel some uncomfortableness around it. The belief may be "I am a good person," and you find that uncomfortable to own. Or the belief may be "I am lonely," and you do not want to admit this.

By owning the belief, you are already starting to shift it to either change it or to own it and grow it. I will provide you with steps as to how to action this so that you are facilitating your growth with your beliefs.

Again, for each of the following: write down the beliefs you get, the very first responses. Your answers will tend to be sentences.

a. **You, yourself**—*what do I believe about me? What do I believe about myself personally?*

b. **Personal growth and development**—*what do I believe about personal growth and development?*

c. **Emotions**—*what do I believe about emotions?*

d. **Happiness**—*what do I believe about happiness?*

e. **Trust**—*what do I believe about trust?*

f. **Relationships**—*what do I believe about relationships?*

g. **What you deserve in life**—*what do I believe I deserve in life?*

h. **Your purpose in life**—*what do I believe about my purpose in life?*

As an example, I am going to jot down the first thoughts that come to my mind as to my beliefs on the first topic:

You, yourself—*what do I believe about me? What do I believe about myself personally?*

- I am strong.

- I don't have many friends.
- Most people judge me.
- Most people can't handle me.
- People are scared of me.
- I am sad that this is the case.
- I have friends and family who love me unconditionally.
- I have wisdom.
- I trust myself.

Step Two: Identify—*Helpful* or *Limiting*

For each topic, go through each of your individual beliefs and identify whether the belief is helpful to you and your growth, or if it is limiting you and your growth. Through identifying this, you can then change the limiting beliefs if you choose to and grow the helpful ones.

Put an H next to the "helpful" ones and an L next to the "limiting" ones. Some beliefs may be helpful and limiting at the same time, so identify which part of the belief is helpful and which part is limiting. Put an H/L next to these beliefs.

Then next to each belief, write down why you believe it is helpful or limiting, so you are clear on your reasoning and process.

Continuing with my above example, this is how you work with this step:

You, yourself—*what do I believe about me? What do I believe about myself personally?*

I am strong—H/L

- Helpful part is I am strong and resilient.
- Limiting part is I may suppress my vulnerability at times because I believe I am strong.

I don't have many friends—L

- Limiting as I am not valuing the friends that I do have and that I am comfortable being with me.

Most people judge me—L

- Limiting as I won't put myself out there or I will not have much to do with people because I am wary of being judged.

Most people can't handle me—L

- Limiting as I may put up a persona, so people can handle who I am or I pretend it does not affect me or I distance myself and stand outside of situations.

People are scared of me—L

- Limiting as I may put up a persona, so that people are not scared of me or I just don't interact with others.

I am sad that this is the case—H/L

- Helpful part is that I can see if I am doing anything to contribute to the limiting beliefs above.
- Limiting part is I may put up a persona to not be judged, not be "scary," and so people can handle me, which impacts me being who I truly am.

I have friends and family who love me unconditionally—H

- Helpful as I am seeing and accepting the love of the people in my life.

I have wisdom—H

- Helpful as I own my wisdom and what I know.

I trust myself—H

- Helpful as I do trust myself and I can continue to develop this.

Step Three: Determine—*True* or *Not True*

Identify if each belief is true or not. Consider the evidence you have that the belief is true or not true. Go through each of the beliefs to see if they are based on fact or your interpretation of facts. Through seeing the facts by looking at the evidence, it helps put things into perspective. You may have made some generalizations because your emotion influenced you in how you felt about things.

An example of how to do this:

You, yourself—*What do I believe about me? What do I believe about myself personally?*

I am strong—H/L

- Helpful part is I am strong and resilient;
- Limiting part is I may suppress my vulnerability at times because I believe I am strong.
- *True*: even when I am vulnerable, I am strong in that I allow myself to feel vulnerable and show it.

I don't have many friends—L

- Limiting as I am not valuing the friends that I do have, and that I am comfortable being with me.
- *Not true*: I have friends that are amazing, and there is no quantity you can put on quality. There are possibly people who view me as a friend, and I don't even know that.

Most people judge me—L

- Limiting as I won't put myself out there, or I will not have much to do with people because I am wary of being judged.
- *Not true*: individuals who have projected their issues onto me judge me. These people are judging themselves, and it actually isn't about me.

Most people can't handle me—L

- Limiting as I may put up a persona, so people can handle who I am or I pretend it does not affect me or I distance myself and stand outside of situations.
- *Not true*: a lot of individuals don't understand me, rather than can't handle me. What is there to handle? Only my truth. When I can't handle someone, it is not them I can't handle; it is myself I can't handle while I am around them.

People are scared of me—L

- Limiting as I may put up a persona, so that people are not scared of me, or I just don't interact with others.

- *Not true*: they are not scared of me. However, I acknowledge in the past this may have been the case. They are scared of the truth or me speaking my truth. In speaking my truth, I share my processing and transparency, which means exposure. For many people, such exposure means they feel vulnerable, so this is what they are scared of, their vulnerability, if they are scared at all.

I am sad that this is the case—H/L

- Helpful part is that I can see if I am doing anything to contribute to the limiting beliefs above.
- Limiting part is I may put up a persona to not be judged, not be "scary," and so people can handle me, which impacts me being who I truly am.
- *True*: I have been sad that people have been scared of me, can't handle me, and judge me. What does this mean? I have been judging and rejecting myself, so I am sad I have done that to myself.

I have friends and family who love me unconditionally—H

- Helpful as I am seeing and accepting the love of the people in my life.
- *True*: they are awesome, and I love them so dearly back.

I have wisdom—H

- Helpful as I own my wisdom and what I know.
- *True*: damn right I do.

I trust myself—H

- Helpful as I do trust myself, and I can continue to develop this.
- *True*: damn right I do.

Step Four: Transform Any Limiting Beliefs to Helpful Beliefs

Identify the beliefs that are limiting that you would like to change. These are the beliefs you labelled L in step two of the process. This also includes the L part of your answer, where you put H/L.

With each limiting belief what you do is create a new helpful belief to replace the limiting one. For example, if you believe, "Emotions are bad," then this belief will limit you because when you feel emotions, you will more than likely suppress them. Changing your belief to "I love emotions" is a massive step to take, and you will more than likely not get there. If you change your belief to "I choose to grow my ability to accept my emotions," then this is a step towards embracing and loving emotions; in turn, you are less likely to suppress them and will be more receptive to working with them.

If you change the new belief to "I will try to …" or "I would like to …," then you more than likely will not change the belief. Why? Because both of these statements at the beginning of a new belief indicate that you are not fully committed to putting the new belief into action. When you say you "tried" to do something, you either did it, didn't do it, or did some action towards it. It is far more empowering to clearly state what you did or didn't do so that you are conscious of your actions. "I would like to" indicates it would be nice to do and one day you will get around to it, but more than likely you won't.

Start your new helpful belief with "I choose to ..." or "I will ..." because these statements have an intention of ownership, commitment, and empowerment, and your subconscious and conscious mind will respond far more effectively.

Continuing with my example, this is how to work through this using my L or the limiting part of my H/L beliefs:

You, yourself—*What do I believe about me? What do I believe about myself personally?*

I am strong—H/L

- Limiting part is I may suppress my vulnerability at times because I believe I am strong.
- *True*: even when I am vulnerable, I am strong in that I allow myself to feel vulnerable and show it.
- *Limiting to helpful belief*: I choose to grow my ability to feel and expose my vulnerability to myself. I choose to see owning and feeling my vulnerability as a strength.

I don't have many friends—L

- Limiting as I am not valuing the friends that I do have, and that I am comfortable being with me.
- *Not true*: I have friends that are amazing, and there is no quantity you can put on quality. There are

possibly people who view me as a friend, and I don't even know that.

- *Limiting to helpful belief*: I choose to accept that the people in my life are the ones that are meant to be in my life, now. And I choose to be open to more wonderful people in my life.

Most people judge me—L

- Limiting as I won't put myself out there, or I will not have much to do with people because I am wary of being judged.
- *Not true*: individuals who have projected their issues onto me judge me. These people are judging themselves, and it actually isn't about me.
- *Limiting to helpful belief*: I choose to accept others have their opinion and I choose to grow my acceptance of myself.

Most people can't handle me—L

- Limiting as I may put up a persona, so people can handle who I am or I pretend it does not affect me or I distance myself and stand outside of situations.
- *Not true*: a lot of individuals don't understand me, rather than can't handle me. What is there to handle? Only my truth. When I can't handle someone, it is not them I can't handle; it is myself I can't handle while I am around them.
- *Limiting to helpful belief*: I choose to grow my acceptance of myself and others.

People are scared of me—L

- Limiting as I may put up a persona, so that people are not scared of me, or I just don't interact with others.
- *Not true*: They are not scared of me. However, I acknowledge in the past this may have been the case. They are scared of the truth or me speaking my truth. In speaking my truth, I share my processing and being transparent, which is being exposed. For many people, being exposed means they feel vulnerable, so this is what they are scared of, their vulnerability if they are scared at all.
- *Limiting to helpful belief*: I choose to manage my emotions in a healthy way and grow my acceptance of myself.

I am sad that this is the case—H/L

- Limiting part is I may put up a persona to not be judged, not be "scary," and so people can handle me, which impacts me being who I truly am.
- *True*: I have been sad that people have been scared of me, can't handle me, and judge me. What does this mean? I have been judging and rejecting myself, so I am sad I have done that to myself.
- *Limiting to helpful belief*: I will honor my emotions, do right by me, and grow my acceptance of what I experience.

Step Five: Act on Helpful Beliefs

This step is about implementing your beliefs, so you have evidence of your growing conscious expression of them. Where you: (1) identify when you are actioning and expressing your helpful beliefs, labelled H, (from stage one of the process) AND (2) give yourself permission to action your new helpful H beliefs.

Stage one helpful H beliefs: with the helpful H beliefs that you identified in stage one of this process, it is important to take the time to reflect on and identify when you express and action them. This will provide you with the tangible evidence of your belief. This builds confidence and supports you to more consciously express the belief in your life so that you can gain the maximum benefits from it.

As I have stated, when you consciously express the belief, it becomes even more powerful. One of my helpful beliefs is "I trust myself." Every time I trust what I know and I take action on that trust, I will consciously acknowledge what I did, why I did it, and that it is another example of how I trust myself. I experience this when I know I am to contact a person by phone, text, email, or messenger. They often respond: "I just needed to hear from you right now," "I was just thinking about you," or "Your timing is always bang on." And in response I say to myself internally, "Go girl, I knew with the person coming to my mind, I was to act on it and contact them, I own I trust myself and my processing."

If required, you may want to do some free writing about the helpful belief to explore it further.

Stage four changing limiting to helpful beliefs: with the new helpful beliefs that are replacing your limiting beliefs, this step requires you to consciously put them into action. This is so that you create the evidence you need to be confident in working with them.

I will use my example from above where I identified the limiting belief, "I don't have many friends." The next time I think or feel this, I will consciously say to myself, aloud or in my head, "That is a belief from my past, and I now choose to let it go. I accept that the people in my life are the ones that are meant to be in my life now." Then I will acknowledge these people and the gifts that they bring me. This is another example of self-facilitating the unravelling of your conditioning.

Another example is my limiting belief, "Most people judge me." The next time this happens, I can say to myself, "Yes, they are judging me, and that is their choice. I choose to accept they have their opinion and I choose to grow my acceptance of myself." If the judgements cause a reaction in me, then it is my issue, and I am judging myself.

Limiting Beliefs Concerning Others

You also have limiting beliefs about other people that you can change to new helpful beliefs. Here's an example of one of my limiting beliefs about someone else: "Isabella [a previous colleague] betrayed me and is untrustworthy." I can't change Isabella, so how can I change my limiting beliefs about her?

What you can do—change how you feel about the person, your emotional attachment to them, and how you respond to them. This is how you can do this.

The belief about my previous colleague Isabella, that she had betrayed me: I chose to work towards changing this belief to a helpful one where I accepted her. I couldn't change her, but what I could change was my view, my feelings, and my beliefs about her. While I had a limiting belief about Isabella, I had an emotional attachment to her, which meant I was still easily affected by her. So if I thought about her, I would feel emotions. When I saw Isabella, I would have reacted based on the belief that she had betrayed me. This would have meant I was still giving my personal power away to her.

The betrayal I experienced was that she'd judged me to other colleagues behind my back. My issue was I had trusted her with what I had shared with her. I recognized feeling betrayed was my issue as I was emotionally needy of her for my safety and security, my trust. Her issue was she was vulnerable about her job, so she expressed these insecurities at my expense.

Working through this limiting belief about Isabella was about me taking back responsibility for my emotional well-being and filling my emotionally neediness to feel safe and secure myself, and not leaving it in someone else's, in this case Isabella's, hands.

Working towards being neutral and accepting of people means you accept where they are at, who they are, and what they do. You are working with healing and releasing the emotional neediness you have of them. The new belief I created about Isabella: "I choose to grow my ability to accept her for what she did and who she is." If I experience any further emotions about Isabella, they are not about her; they will be about me. They are a sign I still have some healing to do and filling of my emotional neediness.

I encourage you to proceed similarly to change your limiting beliefs that involve other people.

Influencing and Changing Your Beliefs

You have identified a few of your beliefs in relation to a range of topics; however, there are so many more yet to be recognized, explored, and either embraced or changed.

To identify more of your beliefs, be aware of your processing both internally and externally. Question yourself as to why you think something, why you are feeling something, why you are about to do or say something, or why you did what you did and said what you said. This will provide you with more awareness as to how your beliefs are influencing and impacting you. Also it will allow you to identify any limiting and helpful beliefs to work with.

About the existing and new helpful beliefs you have— grow their influence in your life. Be aware of how you express them and how they are reflected in what you do and say. The more conscious you are of them, the more powerful they are in their intent. Look for evidence of them being expressed in your life. For example, if you believe you are a good person, be aware of how you express that goodness.

Where the belief is a limiting one, question yourself to recognize where your belief comes from. Identify the layer experience and assess the evidence as to whether the belief is true or not. If you have evidence of the belief being true (from past experiences), know that the experience is what has happened and is in the past. And that you can let it go and have a different experience.

If the beliefs are not yours—you have taken on board other people's beliefs about yourself, others, or situations, and you actually don't believe them—then identify whose they are. Explore why you took them on board and whether you want to keep the beliefs or let them go. These beliefs are not yours to hold onto. If required, identify a new helpful belief to replace the limiting one and put it into action.

If the belief is not yours, then find out what you do believe. Or just let it go and don't carry it around anymore.

If the belief is limiting and yet you have evidence that it is true, test the belief as to the practicalities of it. Put the belief to the side, and look for evidence of the opposite of the belief.

When you have a limiting belief about something or someone, you will have emotions about them. Looking for evidence of the opposite of the belief allows the emotions to balance out and not be so impacting on you. Be open to experiencing something different; then check the belief out afterwards as to whether it is relevant and appropriate anymore.

I was working with a manager, Steve, and he was quite frustrated with his management meetings. He shared his belief that the meetings were ineffective. Emerging from those regular meetings, Steve would carry the frustrated energy, emotion, and approach with him into the meetings with his team of direct reports. The meeting scenario was what triggered his frustration processing.

I asked Steve, "Is there anything effective about your management meetings? Is there anything that is working well?" As he pondered this, the emotional frustration he had been feeling settled, and he became more balanced. Steve identified many elements that were working well in the management meetings, and that it was just the ineffective things that were absorbing him. It was powerful for him to identify the opposite of his belief because he was able to address the ineffective elements of the meeting in a more grounded and non-reactionary manner. From there, he was able to approach the meetings with his direct reports in a more constructive and influential manner.

When you identify beliefs that are limiting you in any area of your life, acknowledge the belief and voice it out loud to process it out of your head and to let it go. Then change it to a new helpful belief.

The limiting belief will reduce your receptiveness and openness to what you experience. You will be closed off in what you see and hear. One of the aims of the new helpful belief is to open up your energy and processing so that you see and hear opportunities that will allow you to have new experiences.

If you have a limiting belief:

- Identify the layer situation it comes from.
- Free write out the situation in full detail to release it, process it out of yourself, and trigger any other mental, emotional, or energy processing.
- Rip up or burn (responsibly, safely, and only in burn season) what you have written to release it.
- Say to yourself, "I have experienced this in the past, and I now choose to let it go and have new experiences."
- Then identify a new helpful belief to replace it.
- Be aware of implementing and expressing the new helpful belief.

You need to truly feel the stages of the above process, not just action it from a speaking head where you are just saying the words. Your intent to experience change through releasing the limiting belief and implementing the new belief needs to be strong, clear, and felt deeply within.

Be aware of the words you use and what you are saying, so you hear the beliefs you have that you may not be aware of. Identify the impact that the belief is having on you and what you experience. Change the language and words you use.

A well-known example of this is where you might say, "I am just a student (or "mother," "stay-at-home father," etc.)." The word "just" immediately indicates a lack of self-worth and that you do not value who you are and what you do. It can be as simple as saying to yourself "I let that go, and I am a . . .." Value yourself at that moment and change the processing.

Be aware of how you share your beliefs with others. Be mindful of not imposing your beliefs on them and impacting them. If you do, this is your neediness. Own your beliefs, rather than express them in general. Then you leave the space for others to own what they believe. "I believe . . ." or "My experience is . . ." Take responsibility for your experience around the belief.

Take time to listen to other people's beliefs, and be open to discovering new information and seeing things differently. Hearing other people's beliefs is an opportunity to check out how much you believe what you believe. If you have a reaction to what they say, this may be an indicator that you have a belief that requires some exploration along with possible judgements, rejection, and expectations you may have.

Where you have generalized beliefs, question them and get specific with them so that you deal with facts and contextualize your belief.

Understanding Others' Beliefs

When people share beliefs with you, and you do not understand them fully, it is important to take time to ask questions so that you can understand. Be aware of not assuming. As we have explored, your past is different to theirs and your interpretation of what they have shared may be different, so check it out.

I have had participants in my programs believe I was judging them. I knew I wasn't; however, I wanted to understand why they believed this, just in case I had and was not aware of it; or so that I could support them.

I would ask, "What is it I said or did that told you I was judging you?" This enabled me to see what they were experiencing through their eyes and understand them. In some cases, they couldn't provide evidence that I was judging them. This enabled them to see their belief and what was really going on for them. Often it was that they were feeling vulnerable and were judging themselves. And they were judging me by saying I was judging them—ahhhhh. In some cases, what was troubling them was what was going on in their lives outside of the training.

Here are some of the types of questions you can ask to gain understanding of others' beliefs:

- Help me understand why you believe that.
- What evidence do you have that that is true?
- Why do you believe that? Where have you experienced that before?
- Why do you think that?
- Why did you do what you just did?
- Can you give me an example?
- What specifically do you mean?
- Can you share more of what your thoughts are about what you believe?

- Where have you experienced that for you to believe that?
- Can you share more of the picture you have?

The number one intention for asking any of these questions has to be because you want to understand. If this is not your intention, don't ask the question.

A check-in—your intentions are part of your attitude. They have mental, emotional, and energy processing attached to them, so people can sense and feel your intentions. Intentions impact trust levels, so if you are not true to your intention, people will pick up on this and it will impact your relationship.

The more you work with your beliefs, the more you will find that you can shift them very quickly. You can experience different outcomes in a very short space of time.

I had a significant moment with beliefs after I moved to Melbourne. I was staying with a friend while I was looking for a place to live. I had been in Melbourne for two weeks. It was Saturday morning, and we went out for coffee. On the way back to the car, I said to my friend, "I'm not going to be able to find anywhere to live." After hearing what I'd said, I voiced to myself out loud, "I let that go, and I am open to finding the place that is right for me." I had a limiting defeatist belief that I'd been carrying around with me.

At the moment of letting go of the belief, I noticed a real estate agency directly opposite where I had parked the car. We went in, and there was a place to rent that was ideal for me. I'd never even noticed the real estate agency when we'd gotten out of the car. My limiting belief had impacted me in being closed off to seeing it. In releasing the belief, I was able to open up to opportunities again and see what was in front of me.

From that day onwards I made a commitment to myself to hear all of the things I was saying, both internally and externally. If I identified any limiting statements or thoughts I had, I would explore where they came from, why I had them, and I would take the steps to let them go. I replaced my limiting statements with ones that were expansive rather than restrictive and ones that supported me being open to all opportunities and to growing and developing.

There are times now when I recognize I have said a limiting belief, and I immediately say, "I choose to let that go." The limiting belief shifts quickly. There are times when I don't need to supplement it with a new helpful belief. And there are times when I do, so that I am clear in the intention I am putting out—clear for myself.

Be aware of you not limiting yourself.

Benefits of Working with Your Beliefs

Being aware of your beliefs helps you to understand yourself and others more. It provides you with insight into behaviors that you demonstrate and what is actually driving them. This supports you to be more accepting.

It is important to be able to identify whether the belief is yours or if you took it on board from someone else because who wants to carry other people's beliefs around for them? Knowing what is true and right for yourself is you standing in your personal power.

Understanding your beliefs will help you to have insight into why others do what they do and say what they say, so you do not personalize things. This can only benefit you as a partner, friend, employer, colleague, or parent.

Knowing how to work with beliefs helps you to change the experiences and the outcomes you have had that no longer serve you, and it supports you to influence your potential to experience new outcomes.

Through understanding other people's beliefs, it will help you to be able to support them changing their behaviors because you will be changing your feelings and behaviors towards them.

Your beliefs influence what you deserve in life and your belief in yourself. By releasing all the limiting beliefs, you become limitless, and your potential is limitless.

And about that opening situation I described concerning my limiting money and business beliefs—I am still currently working with this one. Not the beliefs from that particular situation, but other related ones that have surfaced. As I mentioned, there are layers of beliefs attached to the layers in the layers. Your beliefs are also attached to what you have stored in your subconscious, so like the memories, they will come through at the time you are ready to see, hear, and work with them. Consequently, this is why I have had other ones surface that I can work with.

As we have explored, your beliefs will be attached to emotions, and you can experience emotional reactions in situations where your beliefs are tested and also where your values conflict, your attitude is questioned, your behaviors are rejected, and whenever a similar layer situation presents itself.

Unless you are aware of the conditioned emotional reaction, like my example where I wanted to have a go at the young man who was behaving differently during my program, your reaction will create a similar outcome to the ones you have always experienced, thus reinforcing your beliefs and underlying issues. The key is being able to unravel the conditioning. In the upcoming chapter, you will explore how to do this and develop your ability to respond, instead of react.

CHAPTER 10

RESPONDING RATHER THAN REACTING

"I found it very confusing" are the words I see in Nancy's email. My heart stops. I hold my breath for a moment. This is feedback about the book I have spent many months and hours writing. I am shocked, stunned, and gobsmacked. I was expecting Nancy to tell me, "This is amazing, love the book." I am so so needy of getting this right and it being of value. No, instead quite the opposite. These are the only words I can focus on in the whole email. Oh, I feel such a failure, I feel so damn useless, everything I touch I stuff up, and I can't even get writing a book right.

The one thing in this book process I believed I was certain about was the book, so after getting Nancy's email, it felt like that had been ripped from beneath me. And the person doing the ripping was me. I was so confident in the book and what I had written (or was I?). So I was questioning, "What have I got left now? Where do I go from here?" As tears started welling up in my eyes, I felt deflated and wanted to run away from everything, including life. This is what I was working towards for years, and it was not good enough, so what would I do now?

I called out to Mum and shared Nancy's feedback from the email I'd just read. She immediately went into defending me mode. I so love her for that. I rang my partner, as I was so so needy of reassurance about my book. I don't want it to be the truth. Inside I was screaming, "Please please, please, let this be a dream and be wrong! I can't handle this if this is the truth. I am done, and I give up!"

I knew I was reacting all over the place. In fact, I did such a good job of it that I actually didn't absorb the rest of the information in the email. I was triggered by the word "confusing" and that the book was not yet ready for editing, but rather needed more development. Yet again another trigger that the book and I are not good enough.

One of my past layer situations was creeping up on me from the depths of my subconscious. The suppressed memory, impacts, and processing came rushing to the surface. In that moment, I did not see what was happening as my emotions clouded everything I was thinking, feeling, and my energy. The advantage I did have was that I was aware that I was reacting and I knew how to work with the reaction so that I could explore my conditioning, heal the impacts of my previous experiences, and have a different outcome. And the way for me to change these reactions was for me to respond and make different choices.

You will experience emotional reactions through the hours of your day, during days of the week, and weeks of the year. Your level of awareness around when you are reacting will influence whether you capture the reaction and do something with it before you act on it, or you continue to repeat the layer situations and outcomes from your past.

This chapter explores the nature of reactions themselves, the process you go through when you react, and how you can change your reactions. Some of your reactions will be straightforward in changing, and others may be ingrained and take some conscious work for you to unravel.

There are stages to your reactions, with the external event that triggers the reaction, the internal processing that is triggered, and then your external expression of the reaction. Becoming more familiar with your internal reactions when they are triggered will enable you to change the external outcome. And if you can get to a stage where you recognize the external trigger before you react, then you will be one step ahead in working with what is happening to you internally.

Being Triggered

The phrase often associated with internal reactions and being triggered is "having your buttons pushed." There are lovely people in the world who will go out of their way to endeavor to push your buttons and get a reaction from you. Essentially, they are using it to avoid what they are feeling inside. If they can have power over you, then they can control and have power over the internal processing that they are feeling. They get to suppress what is happening in themselves and protect themselves from their emotions. You could even see their attempts to push your buttons as a compliment being delivered in an interesting and weird way. They view you (subconsciously) as the source of why they are experiencing their feelings. Oh, you powerful thing, you!

Being triggered is where someone does or says something that is similar to what you experienced in past layer situations and the processing that you suppressed back then gets triggered (this is the button) with the emotional and mental impacts being the most prominent. You experience an internal emotional reaction to the situation, combined with a pattern of conditioned words. You then express this reaction in the form of a conditioned behavior. This is the behavior you learned in the past as to how to deal with and express the emotion that has been triggered.

The key element that makes your action a reaction is the emotion attached to it and how the conditioning has become automatic. "Automatic" in that you do not think about what you are doing until after you have done it. There is also no consideration for what the outcome will be because you are caught up in the emotion and processing at the time.

Your past conditioning has got you; it has a hold on you and is influencing what you are experiencing. And generally reactionary outcomes are ones where you will feel you could have done things differently, or you are not happy about them.

Changing Your Reactions

Do you want to be happy about the outcomes you experience? Do you want to take your personal power back and be more true to yourself? Then changing your reactions is imperative so that you cease being at the mercy of the conditioning from your past.

You can change your reactions through unlearning what you have learnt. Your reactions are learned from the environment you grew up in, and what you learned can be different from what even your siblings learned as a reaction. People's reactions can be very different.

For example, we can observe this where two people, Samson and Irwin, are threatened, and they have different reactions, sitting on the spectrum from slightly to extremely different. Irwin may start fighting the person who is threatening him while Samson runs away. A person makes a racist joke in front of them; Samson laughs nervously while Irwin abuses the person for what they said.

You learned your reactions from what was acceptable and not acceptable in your home environment. What others showed and taught you. Your emotional reactionary behaviors are not natural to you; they are conditioned.

I grew up around anger. In my family, if you did not yell and fight back, you got nowhere. It was what I saw my parents do. Then I started protecting my mother from my father's anger, and the fighting then was between him and me. This became my normal.

You may have experienced or are aware of people reacting by crying, withdrawing, and shutting down. Those reactions are more familiar to them because this was what was acceptable in their family environment.

The important thing to know is that **because you learned these reactionary behaviors, you are able to unlearn them.**

And why would you want to unlearn them? They have huge detrimental impacts on you and your life.

Impact of Reactions

Reactions can destroy relationships, jobs, situations, and lives within a split second, not just by what you do but also what you say. Once you react and have spoken the words or demonstrated the behavior, you cannot take it back. Most regrets are about what a person did when reacting. Because in reacting, you allow your emotions to take over and dictate your actions and outcomes.

The emotion can be so overwhelming when you react that you can actually shut down your awareness and consciousness of what you are doing. Then, upon becoming aware again, you can be shocked at what occurred.

When you react, you are allowing other people to influence your life; they can push your buttons and trigger emotions in you, whether they do it intentionally or not. You give your personal power away to them due to your emotional attachment to them, and you are easily baited and emotionally affected by them. Your vulnerability and neediness to be emotionally safe and secure are the prominent issues underlying your reaction.

So the moment you are around someone from your past, they are behaving in the same way they did in the situation that created one of your layers, and you have unhealed emotion and impacts attached to the situation, then it can trigger an emotional reaction. Or when you find yourself in a similar situation to the past layers, it can trigger an emotional reaction. Or you are around other people (you might have only just met them), who look, sound, behave, or have a similar energy to the people from those past layers, it can trigger emotions inside of you.

The trigger for my reactions in that situation described in the chapter's opening was Nancy's word "confusing." I took it personally and as a judgement. This was a similar process to what I had experienced in the past, where at school my speeches, essays, and work was compared to others, and I was never good enough. So I would feel deflated and give up on learning the skills or, where I could, I would change subjects. I felt useless, a failure, and insignificant. Oh—and that I needed lots of work to get it right. This is what surfaced when I read Nancy's email about the book. I was so close to doing what I have done previously, giving up on the book. Giving up on what I loved. Which essentially would be giving up on myself.

When you react, you immediately act on those internally triggered emotions and impacts. You do so without thinking about what you are doing or what the outcome will be because you just want to protect yourself.

Notice in my opening example I immediately contacted the people I felt safe with to fill my neediness for reassurance that the other person was wrong. So now I am judging the other person. As I did not act on my reaction towards Nancy, the limiting impact of my reaction was only experienced by me. In the past, before being aware of my reactions, I would have sent an email to Nancy filled with my reactions, emotions, and energy.

This never worked for me; it got me in strife and made the situations way more complicated. It also hurt and upset others. I was dumping my reactions on them.

There is always an outcome of a reaction, and it will be a limiting and impacting one. Other people are affected by what you say and do. You will feel guilty, beat yourself up, and this will reinforce your layer. You continue to repeat the same pattern of behavior, which continues you experiencing the same outcome.

Most importantly *you* are impacted by the outcome. You know that what you do when you react is not OK. You go against what is the right thing to do and your truth.

Take the situation where you may have just met someone, and you instantly take a dislike to them. A reaction.

How can you instantly not like someone you have just met? There will be some aspect of that person that reminds you of someone from your past. It is triggering the unhealed and unresolved emotion from a layer situation. Your emotion has nothing to do with the person you have just met; it has to do with your past.

You don't feel good about your reaction inside, even if you try to convince yourself that you do through justifying what you did. The truth always surfaces, either internally through you realizing it, or it ends up in your face. The law of cause and effect.

After my reaction about how Nancy read my book, the truth I was running away from came to the surface. I was able to recognize that when I emailed the book to her, in my subconscious and slightly in my conscious mind, I had questions about some of the chapters, the order of the chapters, and I had my fingers crossed behind my back. I was hoping it was OK, however I did not actually truly know it was OK. So Nancy actually gave me a gift.

Reactions are emotionally triggered actions, expressed with little awareness of what you are doing. You don't often think about what you have done until after the outcome. Your behaviors were conditioned to protect you from hurt and so that you do not experience the layer situations again. They also keep you protected from your truth and the truth.

When you react, you give your personal power away. You give away your ability to influence the outcomes you experience in life, and you give others the ability to dictate what you will experience through your emotional attachment and reactions to what they say and do.

If I had followed through with my reaction to the email, I would have given up on what you are reading now. And I know I would have spent the rest of my life with so many past what-ifs, guilt, judgements, and regrets.

There are other ways to process your emotions, manage yourself, and change your behaviors. As you heal the emotional, mental, and other impacts attached to the layers, you find you cease reacting, as there is nothing to be triggered, so your behavior is different.

The key here is to develop your ability to respond rather than react. The responding process requires you to be conscious of capturing the internal emotional triggers so that you can work with them internally before you do anything externally. To know the steps required to respond, it is important to know how the reactionary process works.

THE PROCESS OF REACTING

Throughout your day there is always something happening and going on around you. And you internalize this through hearing it, seeing it, smelling it, feeling it, and participating in it.

And if what is happening is similar to the layer experiences you have had in the past, you will experience an internal reaction. It might be a thought, "What a dick head!" or "What the f..k?" It could be heart palpitations, a clenched stomach, or butterflies.

What is being triggered is the unhealed emotions and other impacts from one of your past layer situations. You can feel hurt, angry, vulnerable, needy, guilty, shameful, rejected, or abandoned, as some of the emotions that are triggered.

My nephews, who are in their late teens and early twenties, termed it as "triggered." You have been triggered. This is the name their generation gives this process. Wow, how we have evolved.

My internal reaction to Nancy's email was physiological in that I held my breath and it felt like my heart stopped. The mental processing reflected the emotions I was feeling—guilt for not getting it right and believing I got it wrong; self-rejection in that I was useless; and vulnerable in that I exposed myself and my writing and I was judged (my interpretation of it). Then hurt because I had an emotional attachment to the person's opinion, shame that my writing was not good enough, neediness for reassurance to feel safe and secure. Just to add to it self-doubt in my ability to write, lack of self-belief in that I was not trusting I have the ability to express myself effectively, and lack of self-worth in that I believed I was not good enough. What a bundle to work with!

If you are not aware of your internal reaction, your subconscious mind will override your processing, and you will act on the emotional reaction. You will do or say something without thinking about what the outcome will be. You instantly and automatically behave in a conditioned way and are unaware of what you have done or said until after the outcome.

Some of the reactions you express can be out there and also very subtle. They all are mentally and emotionally impacting. For example: withdrawing, silent treatment, closing off, being the good girl or boy, submitting, taking the blame, being nasty, or hanging up the phone. Also yelling, shouting, retaliating, swearing, sabotaging, belittling, expressing sarcasm, and lying.

Then there are the physically impacting reactions that hurt you, other people, and items. Throwing things, biting, spitting, breaking things, kicking, arson, and crime. As well as anorexia, bulimia, and over-eating. And self-harm, murder, and suicide.

You can also turn to things like drinking, drunk driving, drugs, sex, gambling, shopping sprees, or sniffing solvents. Then you can be very creative with your reactions like putting blue loo in the shampoo, sugar in the petrol tank, spitting in the dinner, and apple pie the bed.

Your reactions can also be expressed in your physical behaviors, such as nervousness, leg twitching, nail-biting, blinking, nose twitching, and scratching. Let's not forget this one—crying (for the intention of emotional blackmail to get a reaction from the other person).

I am sure you have seen and experienced additional reactions to these. What is important is being aware of and working with your own reactions. Take a moment to ponder what it is you do when you react.

You know right down deep in the bottom of your belly that this is not the right thing to do. You cannot take back what you have said or done after you have reacted; it is in the past. There is an impact on others, on yourself, and/or on objects, and there is an outcome that you cannot change. Some of the outcomes that result from reactions are the loss of friendship, breaking of an item or bone, the destruction of property, being sacked from a job, or ending up unconscious or dead.

You can also continue to react again, and the cycle goes on.

You feel guilty as a result of what you have done. You may feel shame, embarrassment, and sadness. What you do then is find yourself blaming the other person or things. You use excuses or justifications: "I have had a bad day at work" or "I am having a bad hair day." You avoid the situation, person, or completely deny what you did or that it even happened.

When I had my reaction about the feedback I received on the book, I wanted to ignore and avoid Nancy, and this was not appropriate. She had taken the time to work on the book. I knew I could work through my reaction, and avoiding was not what I wanted to do anymore even though I wanted to say, "Stuff this." So instead I sent an email thanking her for the feedback and that I would process it. I used as few words a possible, so I did not repeat my old pattern. I gave myself time to work with myself, uncover my truth, and look at my options. This was me changing part of my reaction from previous times.

If you find yourself feeling satisfied with reacting and what you have done, then you are likely trying to justify your reaction. There have been times in my life when I have reacted by letting loose on a person and giving them a "what for." I then justified it by pointing out all the things they had done to me that warranted them deserving the bullets from my mouth. How wrong I was! How do I know? I felt the guilt later.

When you feel good about something that you know is wrong, you are suppressing the guilt and going into denial. The guilt will surface at some time. In a quiet moment when you have nothing to distract yourself with, it surfaces. Sadly for some people, their guilt and truth come to the surface on their deathbed.

If you are reacting and doing any of this, then you:

- do not take responsibility for yourself, your emotions, your actions, and your life;
- give your personal power away so that others and things influence the outcomes of your life, and not you; and
- allow life to happen at you.

I used to be, and still can be in some moments, the "ever-ready reactionary bunny." You only had to look at me in a particular way, and I would react: "What are you looking at?" Or someone would say something, and I would read so far into what they said that I had gone to the outer limits of the universe and back. People would comment, "What on earth are you on about?" My mum used to say, "I am scared of saying anything because of your reactions." My emotions colored everything I heard, saw, felt, and sensed.

As a corporate trainer and facilitator of work readiness programs, I was a fantastic target for participants who wanted to avoid themselves by baiting me. They had their fishing rods out, and I was their catch every time. Their way of dealing with the self-doubt and vulnerability they felt within themselves was to focus their attention on me. If I reacted, they could avoid what was happening in themselves.

The interesting part of being an expressive reactionary person was I set myself up to be blamed for things. My reaction was the visible part of the process, so people remembered what I said or did. They tended not to remember what the other person said or did, the person that triggered the emotional reaction. The reason they remembered the visible behavior, besides it being visible, is that it more than likely connected to some layer experience they'd had. So they had an emotional reaction to my emotional reaction, and they wanted to protect themselves.

I worked tirelessly to change my reactions. The more I healed my emotions and consciously worked with responding rather than reacting, the more I was able to respond to participants baiting me. I would respond to their fishing comments, by saying, "What reaction are you looking for, as I am happy to oblige?" Generally the impact of this was they were silent and not sure where to go with what they were trying to achieve.

Some of the participants in my I Make a Difference program grew up dealing with issues by fighting. In exploring moving from reacting to responding, they expressed, "What do you want me to do while someone is bashing the hell out of me or standing there with a gun in my face? Do I just stand there and take it and say to them, 'Please can you stop for a moment, while I respond to you?'"

My response was that any physical vulnerability is very real; you can get hurt or die. The good old saying, "Sticks and stones will break my bones," yes, they will. So look at what you can do, so you don't get yourself into these situations. If you do end up in these types of situations, then consciously make a choice if you are going to react.

Consciously react, be aware of what you do and aim for the outcome that you want. If the outcome is one that you will not be happy with, then accept that this was your choice, you contributed to the outcome, and take responsibility for it. Don't complain if you beat the crap out of someone, and then you end up in jail, or you have the crap beaten out of you. This choice was in your hands and is your responsibility.

I used to believe fighting was the way to deal with things. I was getting physically hurt by this, let alone the emotional process. I discovered it took far more strength to walk away from a volatile situation than it did to fight. In walking away, I took my personal power back because I chose to look after myself and not put energy into something that was not worth it, and I got a good outcome for myself.

If someone calls you names and you experience some emotional vulnerability, remember the saying, "Words will never hurt me." Words will not hurt you physically; they can only hurt you emotionally if you choose for them to hurt you and only if you are needy of the other person for your emotional well-being. Don't buy into the other person's words and issues.

If what they are saying is judgmental, then this is their issue that they are projecting onto you. Ponder on what you want to have as an outcome. Saying nothing means that you do not take up the responsibility for what they have said; it stays with them. You can walk away from these situations; however, if you do, don't do it out of avoidance because then you are reinforcing a layer and suppressing an aspect of yourself. Walk away for the intention of looking after yourself.

You have the power in your hands to change how you want to express your emotions and what outcomes you want in your life. If you heal your emotions, you will not experience any more emotional internal reactions, so you will not be expressing any external reactions. You will be aware, make choices, and respond to life.

Understanding and implementing the steps to responding is essential in order to make this happen.

THE STEPS TO RESPONDING

Responding is the approach for working with your internal reactions so that you change how you manage them and express them, which in turn changes the outcome you experience. Even what you deem a small change is a change and a move in the right direction to where you are not reacting.

When I reacted to the feedback about my book, my awareness of my internal processing made it possible for me to respond and do things differently. My initial email reply was prompted by me being conscious of not running away, keeping the email short and not saying too much, and giving myself time to process, while respecting Nancy. I also reminded myself that one of the reasons I was experiencing this situation was for my limiting beliefs about being useless and all the other processing to surface. This was an opportunity for me to work with unravelling it and healing it. This situation was happening for extremely beneficial reasons.

Responding involves being aware of your internal reactions. Consciously making choices about how you will manage your emotional reactions and how you will change the outcomes you have experienced in the past to new ones that support your self-worth and self-empowerment.

The difference between reacting and responding is, instead, of acting on the internal emotional reaction immediately, you pause, take your focus and awareness inside of yourself, and work with the reaction. You have not acted on the reaction externally, and you have not expressed any behavior. You are self-facilitating the processing of your reaction internally so that you can make choices as to how you will respond and act externally.

Let's look at what I term "The Five Steps to Responding" (rather than reacting):

1. Awareness
2. Acknowledgment
3. Acceptance
4. Options and Choices
5. Action

To explore the five steps I will work through the example I shared in the opening of this chapter.

Step One

AWARENESS—you take your awareness inside yourself and capture your internal emotional reaction, what your thoughts are, and what you are feeling (emotionally, mentally, energy-wise, and physically).

The physiological impacts of my reaction were changes in my breathing, heart rate, energy, and tightness in my chest. I felt scared, hurt, and deflated. The story I made up was a wonderful drama, and my self-talk and judgements were significant: "I am useless," "I am a failure."

Step Two

ACKNOWLEDGMENT—you acknowledge your internal emotional reaction by asking yourself questions to understand what the feeling is, what the emotions are about, and where they come from.

I explored what I was feeling, and there was an extensive array of emotions with the most absorbing being rejection, shame, and neediness. I identified where the feelings and words came from in my past. Which layer experience? It was school. I was compared to others and given feedback that my work was not of the same standard.

Step Three

ACCEPTANCE—you make your internal emotional reaction OK. You stop fighting what you are feeling and thinking. The reaction belongs to a boy or girl inside yourself at the age you were from the past layer and there is unhealed emotion attached to it (don't judge yourself or make this wrong).

I took time to sink into the emotions and feelings and be with them, knowing this was meant to happen and that it would be OK. I did not fight what I was thinking and feeling. I embraced what I was experiencing as an opportunity for my growth.

Step Four

OPTIONS AND CHOICES—you look at what outcome you want. In reacting you don't think about the outcome until after it has happened. With responding you explore what outcome you want, so your intention is clear, as this will guide your actions. You look at what options you have as to how you express your internal reaction externally. Then you choose the option that will achieve your outcome.

I gave myself time to ponder on what I did want to do in this situation, and I processed out my emotions. I made a choice to continue with the book. I wanted to find a way forward where I could express myself to the best of my ability. I wanted to do the best I could for myself, which would be the best for my readers. So I decided to take up the offer of talking with Nancy and face receiving her feedback. I wanted to understand what she shared in the email, explore what needed to be worked on, and find a solution for moving forward and completing the book.

Step Five

ACTION—having made a conscious choice around how you want to respond, you take action.

Four days later I spoke with Nancy and gained clarity as to what I should do to revise the book. I was buzzing. The bizarre thing was that what she shared with me, most of it I already knew and had not applied it in the book; in fact,

I had trained people in some of the approaches. What was also really cool is that I did not judge myself or have any reactions. In fact, I was excited because I had moved to a different place in my growth. The outcome and gift I gained from Nancy and the experience is that I identified that I had become conditioned in my explanation of the processes from delivering the I Make a Difference program. However, this was not a training program but a book for readers. Realizing this enabled me to let go of my conditioning, free myself up, and explore how could I share this information for the reader. A process that is similar and yet so different and a new way of expressing things. Oh and I can't forget this one—I am not useless.

The intention of the five steps is to change the outcomes you experienced in the past to new outcomes. You develop your ability to make choices and take action that is responsive rather than reactive, which creates new outcomes where you do right by you and that you feel good about.

When you respond, you:

- take your personal power back; you take responsibility for yourself, your emotional well-being, and your truth;
- make conscious choices to influence the outcomes in your life; and
- grow, develop, and accept each step you take no matter how small or big it is. You see the difference in each outcome from the last outcome you experienced, and you know you are doing right by you.

STAGES TO RESPONDING

You may be wondering, "How on earth do I go from some of the ingrained reactions I have to where I respond?" There are different stages you will experience as you grow your ability to respond rather than react.

The most important aspect of developing your ability to move from reacting to responding is to recognize, be aware of, and acknowledge every tiny to large step you take. Be aware of the difference in everything that you have done and said, how you feel, how others react or respond, and how the outcome has changed from previous reactionary situations.

If you only focus on how things are the same as the past and not see what is different, you will keep reinforcing the layer and the reactionary behavior. However, if you identify what you have done differently and what is different, then you will have a foundation to continue to build on. Your self-belief and trust in your ability to change the outcomes of your life will continue to grow. It is important that you have evidence of the changes you are making to reinforce that you are on the right track.

While you are healing the emotions from each of your layers, there will still be people, words, energies, behaviors, and situations that you will have internal emotional reactions to. Some of your layer reactionary behaviors will shift and change very quickly, and some will take a bit longer. There will be some very entrenched reactions attached to thick layers that may take time, awareness, acceptance, and processing to heal and dissolve. These types of layers may mean the conditioning of the reactionary behavior may require more focus, energy, and time to unravel.

The important point is that this is a process, and the process has its own natural life to it. If you try to control it, you will delay the progress of the process. If you have expectations as to how it will unfold, you are controlling it, and you will get in the way of the process. Accept your growth as it unfolds and be aware if you start doubting it. If you do know this is a conditioned part of your processing, what you can do is ask yourself, "What did I do well?" and "What can I do differently next time?"

In moving from reacting to responding you may find there are times where you:

1. react and then become aware of the reaction after the outcome and then you respond;
2. react and halfway through expressing the reaction, you become aware of what you are doing, and then you respond;
3. react internally, and respond externally; or
4. no internal reactions

Stage One: React, and After the Outcome, Respond

You are faced with a situation that is similar to a previous layer experience, and what you suppressed gets triggered. You have an internal emotional reaction, and you react externally. Too late you've said it and done it, and now you have an outcome you know is not right and that you are not happy with. And you contributed to it because of your reaction.

Know this—you can still respond, even after the outcome. Do not walk away from the situation with a reactionary outcome.

You have the choice of either acting immediately or within a reasonable timeframe after the outcome where you can act on a response. The important intention behind you responding is that you ultimately walk away from the person or situation taking responsibility for yourself, your life, and doing what you know is right by you and the right thing.

I met a supervisor of a team, Ben, who reacted regularly. He attended the I Make a Difference program, and one of the areas he worked with very consciously and studiously was growing his ability to respond, heal his emotions, and reduce his level of reactionary behaviors.

One morning at work, Ben was struggling with what was happening, and an employee came to talk to him. He snapped at the employee. The employee walked away feeling rather emotional, and his self-worth was impacted. When Ben shared his story with me, I asked him, "What did you do next?"

He answered, "Nothing, I just felt guilty."

I then asked him, "What did you want to do?"

He answered, "I wanted to go and apologize to the employee," but he hadn't.

Don't hold back, if an apology is sitting there for you, go and follow through on it, owning what you have done.

If you are going to say sorry, own what you are sorry for and why you reacted: "I am sorry for the tone I used. You did not deserve that. I had other things on my mind, and it was not anything you did." This ensures you are transparent and truthful with yourself. You take responsibility for your process, and this supports you to let go of your self-judgement and move on.

If the other person accepts the apology, then great, growth for both of you and you are both responding. If the other person does not accept your apology, they are likely to be reacting, so you should make this OK. It is their issue and for them to work through their reaction, not for you to do so. The key is for you to take responsibility for yourself and do what you know is the right thing to do.

Stage Two: React and Halfway Through— Respond

In stage two, you have been working on being more aware of your reactions; however, they can be overwhelming and absorbing. You find you have an internal reaction to something, and you act on it straightaway. But in the middle of you reacting and what you are doing or saying, you become aware that you are reacting.

At this point give yourself permission and make it OK to cease reacting right then and there. Put the brakes on.

You have the chance at that moment to respond rather than react.

You may be yelling at someone when you notice you are reacting. You can stop yelling and say to the person, "Sorry, I am reacting, and I apologize. I need to go and take a breather, and I will be back." Or if you know what the reaction is about, own it, and say, "Sorry, I am reacting. I had anger come up that was connected to some of the words you used, and the anger is not at you. It reminded me of something I experienced in the past."

What is powerful about doing this is you are taking responsibility for yourself, your emotions, and your actions at that moment. The apology is for the other person because they did not deserve your reaction, and it is also for yourself.

You are apologizing to yourself for what you have done to yourself in that moment and as a result of the past layer. You have taken your personal power back because you have taken ownership of what you are experiencing and doing. You now have choices as to how you will process any remaining reaction in a way that benefits you.

The key is to walk away feeling good. Feeling good about yourself and about what you have done or said. Only you can change your life.

Stage Three: React Internally and Respond Externally

In stage three, while you still have emotions to heal, you will experience internal reactions. You have grown your ability to know and work with your reactions. Then a situation arises that you internalize, and you have an internal reaction. This time you respond to your reaction internally and then externally.

You capture the internal reaction the moment it is triggered and immediately apply the five steps. And you identify what you are experiencing and where it comes from. As well you make the impacts you are processing OK through not fighting them, but rather accepting them. You make conscious decisions about what outcome you want, what options you have, and what you will express externally. You respond externally demonstrating different behaviors and creating new outcomes for yourself.

I remember the time when some of my program participants were on their "fishing trip" and baiting me. I became very aware that I had an internal reaction. My first conscious response to the reaction was the thought, "This is mainly their issue, not mine." I implemented the five steps and got clear that I did not want to put any energy into their behaviors, and I still wanted to respect them. So I chose to just sit, look at them, listen to what they were saying, and say nothing. There was nothing to say to what they had done and said. The outcome: it all fell a bit flat for a moment, and then we got back to what we were doing. Ohhhh, it felt so good in that moment that I had been able to change a pattern of reacting that had been with me for a long time.

Stage Four: No Internal Reactions

While you still have unhealed emotions from your past layers, you will still experience internal reactions. Once you have healed all of your emotions, you will not experience any more internal or external reactions, as there is no emotion or impacts to be triggered.

The ultimate place to get to is having no internal reactions, as you have fully dissolved the layers.

Rest stop: Being aware of when you are reacting, the types of reactions you experience and when you are responding instead, is a powerful starting point for growing your ability to respond rather than react. The following activity provides you with an opportunity to develop your awareness in this area.

<u>Self-Facilitation Activity—Reactions and Responses</u>

In your notebook or Personal Processing Workbook, spend time free writing your responses to each of the following questions.

a. What type of reactions do you have these days?
b. For each of the reactions you express, ask yourself the following:
    - How do they impact other people?
    - How do they impact you?
c. What are the situations that previously you reacted to but currently you respond to? Describe the previous reaction.

    d. What did you do to change the reaction to a response?

    e. Which of the current reactions that you experience (see first question) do you want to focus on to grow your ability to respond?

Layers of Processing to Your Reactions

While you do still experience reactions, you will have other processing besides emotions that come with reacting. In chapter 8, Integration of You, you explored the five different areas of impacts for healing each of your layers: the mental, emotional, physical, energy, and spiritual areas. When you have a reaction, you will experience processing in most of these areas. Being aware of the healing that takes place for each of these processes is important so that you are clear on what you are experiencing at the time.

In the opening of chapter 8, Integration of You, I shared an example of when I felt angry with my partner Alan because I believed he was not listening to me and then I reacted. I went on to explain that I experienced no emotional or physiological feelings; instead, it was purely residue mental processing, words that were going through my head. And as they were only words, there was very little energy behind the reaction, so it petered out. This was really empowering, as I had immediate evidence of the integration process taking place, and I had the tools to work with the mental impacts. The focus was on my processing and how I was different internally, which is evidence of how I was healing and growing.

Consciously Choosing to React

There have been times where I have chosen to consciously react. I have reacted responsively. This is about reacting with awareness, choice, and self-responsibility.

This is where you experience emotions being triggered attached to a past layer, and you consciously choose to act in a reactionary way. You choose to act on the emotions you are experiencing. You do so fully aware of what you are doing and what the outcome will be. You do this prepared to totally take responsibility for the outcome and accept the outcome. There is no going back on this one.

I do encourage you not to take action like my following example as I could have been significantly hurt, if not even killed, and I would not choose to act on this again. It is MY example of what consciously choosing to react involves.

When I was meeting Simon, I touched him on the shoulder as a friendly gesture. I was not aware that he had had surgery on that shoulder. Simon had been trained in various disciplines to defend himself. He put his finger on my arm in response, or rather reaction, to my touch. The pain I felt was unbelievable. He apologized, saying it was his training going into effect that caused him to react that way. I ended up feeling physically scared of him. He then said a few times to me, "Don't push me because I can't control what I will do." I did not want to live in fear of this threat, as I had lived in fear of physical violence in my childhood.

I had a few run-ins with Simon. One day he went off about something in my house and slammed my door (yes, notice the wording—*my* house, *my* door). I had lots of anger triggered. I made a conscious choice at that moment that I was prepared to get in his face, and I was prepared that he may hurt me significantly, and if that happened, I would take responsibility for my part in it.

I got in his face, and I let loose a barrage of words. I challenged him to hurt me given that that is what he kept saying he didn't want to do, yet it felt like he did.

Simon backed down, but even more importantly I stopped being scared of him. I got to see that in fact he could manage what he did physically, and I let go of the fear that I had held onto from my childhood. This did not mean that I did not believe his words anymore; I still was aware he could hurt me. The difference now was that I was not scared while I was around him; now I was aware. There is a very big difference.

While I was scared, I was suppressing and protecting myself. While I was aware, I stood in my personal power knowing I had choices.

I have also done this in what I wanted to say to a person, well aware it could end the relationship. This was the outcome, and I did not blame that person. I took responsibility for my part in it and that I could have done it differently, but it was what was right for me at the time. I was not able to apologize to the person's face, but I put the energy out there to them with the apology.

Make Conscious Choices

When others react to you, you will be conscious that either you did something purposely to trigger the action—yes, you are one of those fishermen I talk about; or what you have done, said, look like, sound like, or feel like reminds them of one of their past layer situations.

If you have a reaction to their reaction, then you are triggering each other and you know the process for addressing your reaction. If possible, respond and make choices. If you don't have a reaction, then I encourage you to be accepting and supportive of the other person. Be aware of not taking their reaction on board and personalizing it. You could even ask them questions to support their processing. However, please only do this if they are open to it, do not impose your emotional neediness for them to understand themselves on them.

Whether you react or respond, make sure that you do what you know is right by you and the right thing. Make a conscious choice.

If you react and apologize, make sure you truly mean it and that you are saying it first and foremost for yourself. If you don't mean it, then you will be lying, and what you put out there, you get back. Most importantly you are lying to yourself.

If your apology is not genuine, you will find that you still continue to do the same thing and won't change in this area. This will mean you keep experiencing the same outcome.

In apologizing to people be specific about what part of what you did or said you are sorry for. Many times I have not been sorry for what I have said rather how I said it. I have been sorry for the tone I used and the energy I put out.

The importance of clarifying this is for you to gain clarity and take ownership of your process. This assists you to grow your awareness and ability to self-facilitate yourself.

If you choose to react physically, be fully aware of the potential outcomes of your actions. If you kill someone, how are you going to feel and what will be the outcome for you? How are you going to feel about a family that has lost someone? How are you going to feel when you are locked away for a part of, if not the rest of your life? Will you allow someone else to have contributed to you experiencing this? What if you are the one that is maimed or dies?

Physical violence is not the way to go, and I do encourage you to walk away. Having a physical fight is about being vulnerable and needy. It is about feeling so powerless in your ability to influence the other person verbally or emotionally. It is about feeling hurt and wanting to hurt another so that you fill your neediness of being In control, having influence and power, because you feel so vulnerable and Insecure. So you resort to hurting them physically.

The outcomes you experience in life are influenced by what you choose to do. Pause and be conscious of your choices.

What will help you grow your awareness of your choices and assist you to develop your ability to respond is really understanding and being able to apply the five steps. The next chapter continues the exploration of the approach and processing for each of the steps. The five steps are one of the most important tools for self-facilitating the unravelling of your conditioning and the healing and developing of yourself. Embracing the five steps and making them a part of you will enable you to gain benefits from them in every area of your life.

CHAPTER 11

MORE ON THE FIVE STEPS

Mum is finally off the phone. We sit down to have a catch-up and she shares she was speaking to Lisa. We have known Lisa and her family for years. Lisa has a son, Tim, who is a year older than me, and we sort of mixed with the same people in high school. However, we were not close. Tim lives overseas and has done extremely well for himself.

Mum shares what Lisa has been up to and how Tim is doing. Then she says, "Tim is so wonderful to his mother. He pays for her to fly to see him regularly, and he takes her to dinner and on adventures. He is so good to his mother."

Clunk. At that moment my whole body went rigid. I was holding my breath in the middle of my chest, I had a knot in my stomach, and I immediately acted on my reaction. I raised my voice. Words and energy spilled forth from my mouth, "So I am not good enough as a daughter because I don't do those things for you?"

Mum was shocked and taken back, so she shut down and walked away.

I was left brewing in my own emotional crap, wanting to lash out at her, because yet again I felt everyone else was better than me in what they did for people. It didn't matter what I did, no one acknowledged me, and it was never enough. Or so the story in my head that I made up was telling me.

I was having a reaction and I knew it and I hated myself for it. I knew I needed to work with it. This pattern had gone on for too long, and it was not benefiting me, my mother, or our relationship. I was pushing her away when I wanted quite the opposite to happen. Let alone what I was doing to myself, repeating the same old pattern. I was making an assumption about what she was saying and not even understanding her.

And I had an emotional attachment to this type of situation and the words, one I wanted to take responsibility for and change. Time to work with the five steps to unravel this conditioning and heal this part of myself that kept reacting. Why? Because I wanted to for me.

Applying the five steps to responding enables you to make a significant difference to yourself and your life. You are able to identify that the reactions you are experiencing internally in the situation actually have nothing to do with what is happening currently; they have everything to do with your past experiences. Working through the steps provides you with the ability to look at how you can unravel and heal the impacts of your past and make choices, so you have a new experience that is different to the one you have always had.

You will explore the expanded process of the five steps to responding in this chapter, delving more in-depth as to what each step involves, the questions to ask, and the processing required to journey through the five-step process.

The five steps can be applied in any situation, whether you experience a reaction or not. They are the rocks and mortar to you self-facilitating your process, growing your ability to respond, and integrating all aspects of yourself. It is the approach that enables you to understand, heal, reclaim, and develop yourself. And the steps are interwoven into every area of the I Make a Difference Onion Model.

How the Five Steps Come Together

You can only develop yourself and change your life if you are **aware** of yourself and what is happening to you in any given situation. The five steps raise your awareness of your behaviors, internal processing, emotions, what you do to yourself and others, what benefits you, and where you are limiting yourself.

Acknowledging what you are aware of enables you to process and understand what is happening within yourself. This is achieved by identifying what it is that you are experiencing, why you are experiencing it, where it comes from, and recognizing the impact it is having on you.

The acknowledgment process involves asking yourself questions to explore and understand your processing, which develops your ability to self-facilitate and find answers within yourself.

Acceptance of what you are experiencing and the answers you discover supports you to be open to look at how you can do things differently and change things.

Being able to look at all the possible ***options and choices*** to heal and develop who you are and change how you express yourself and how you approach what is happening comes from having specific tools, ways, and processes to choose from.

Taking ***action*** to respond rather than react is totally up to you. Doing something about what you are aware of and changing the patterns in your life is influenced by how you view and feel about things. As well as how you behave and respond to yourself, situations, and others. The five steps put into perspective and make sense of what you experience.

THE FIVE STEPS TO RESPONDING RATHER THAN REACTING

1. Awareness
   - Inside of Yourself
   - Outside of Yourself
   - General Awareness
2. Acknowledgment
3. Acceptance
4. Options and Choices
5. Action

Step One: AWARENESS

Being aware of yourself, what is going on inside of yourself, what is happening for yourself, and what you are doing and saying is the starting point of change. How can you know what to work with if you are not aware of it?

Awareness is about where you put your focus and attention. It is about being conscious, mindful, and observant of all that is going on inside of and around you.

To be able to heal and dissolve the layers of your past and discover your jewel within requires developing your awareness of what you are experiencing internally. This is so you know when you have memories coming from your subconscious mind to your conscious mind, and that the impacts of these memories are being triggered as you are having an internal reaction.

Human beings generally are more aware of what is going on around and outside of them, rather than internally. We are conditioned through being told, "Watch out for that!," "Look out for this!," "Look at what you are doing!" It is easier to be aware of what is going on outside of ourselves too because it is tangible and visible.

Being aware of what is going on inside of yourself can be scary. What might you discover—emotions, the truth, and who you truly are. Your healing and development process requires you being aware of what is going on inside of yourself so that you can work with this process and change how you express yourself externally and the experiences you have outside of yourself.

Aware Inside of Yourself

This requires you to grow your awareness inside yourself as to what you are feeling (physically, emotionally, and energy-wise), thinking, sensing, seeing, hearing, saying, smelling, touching, tasting, and knowing. In turn, you will grow your awareness of your truth, your connection to your jewel, and your amazing qualities and attributes.

Developing your awareness of what you are processing and experiencing internally allows you to capture your reactions internally and work with them before acting externally.

As you expand and deepen your awareness internally, you naturally become more aware externally.

Aware Outside of Yourself

Then as your awareness outside of you grows, you become more aware of what you and others say and do, and what is not said and done. You gain awareness of the patterns, issues, and outcomes that you experience, as well as the messages you get from the environment and generally what is happening around you.

Your General Awareness

Growing your awareness requires you to focus your attention for periods of time on certain aspects and processes within yourself. This will support you to be more familiar with what you experience in your processing in these areas.

You may develop your awareness inside of yourself through initially focusing on one area. Such as exploring your emotions—becoming familiar with what they feel like, look like, sound like, and how they are expressed physiologically and energy-wise, so that you can identify when you experience emotions more easily and quickly. Then move to your mental, your physical, and your energy processing.

The next stage is to develop your ability to be aware of two different areas of processing at the same time. For example, simultaneously focusing on your emotions and your physical self to become "multi-aware." Next, progressing to focusing on three areas within yourself at the same time. Again, the aim for doing this is developing, deepening, and broadening your awareness of your whole self in all areas.

You may initially only focus internally and then grow your focus externally. Then you grow your ability to focus both internally and externally at the same time.

I often take the opportunity when someone asks me, "How are you?" to stop and be aware of all areas of my processing as to how I am. This includes how I am feeling emotionally, physically, energy-wise, what my thought processing has been, and how my life has been recently and why. I don't necessarily provide all of this information in response to the person's question, as it may not be relevant to them. When I do share my processing, I am very clear that I am doing it for me and the growth of my self-awareness.

I also work with being aware of one or many processes at once, internally and externally. This is for the purpose of growing and expanding my awareness.

The more you work with developing your levels of awareness, the more natural they become. They are a part of you. You are able to hear, see, and sense things externally while being aware of what is going on inside of yourself at the same time.

Awareness Example

In the example I shared at the beginning of the chapter where I got upset with my mum, I was committed to changing how I managed these situations. I was going to work with my reactions and develop my ability to respond by applying the five steps.

When mum shared, "Tim is so wonderful to his mother. He pays for her to fly to see him regularly and he takes her to dinner and on adventures. He is so good to his mother," I noticed at that moment that I had an internal reaction to what mum said. So, I took my awareness inside of myself to become aware of what my reaction was. I became aware of my emotional, physical, and mental processing to find: I was holding my breath in the middle of my chest, I had a knot of energy blocked in my stomach, and I went rigid. The words in my head were yelling, "So I am not good enough as a daughter because I don't do those things for you!" In this way I was AWARE of what was happening inside myself.

I had options as to what I could do about what I'd become aware of:

1. I could react and have a go at my mother, dumping my issues on her (which is what I have done previously and did in this situation).
2. I could suppress the knot in my stomach and the words in my head, and pretend they were not

there, thus suppressing and protecting myself (only so they surface again at a later stage).

3. I could move to the next of the five steps, which is where I would ACKNOWLEDGE the knot in my stomach, the holding of my breath, the rigidity of my body, and the words in my head.

Step Two: ACKNOWLEDGMENT

It is great being aware of what is happening with you because understanding what you are aware of provides the information you require to know what you are dealing with. The second step of the five is acknowledgment. This is where you acknowledge what you are aware of.

You recognize the reaction through identifying it, exploring it, processing it, and understanding what you are experiencing. You process why you are experiencing it and where it has come from. You put a name to the reaction. The way to approach the acknowledgment step is by self-facilitating your process and asking yourself questions.

Acknowledgment Example

Continuing with the example with my mother, I was AWARE I had a knot in my stomach and held energy in my chest, so I could take my focus to where these physiological impacts were within myself and ask myself questions:

Question: What am I feeling?
This is about identifying the emotions that are being experienced in the reaction.

My answer: rejection, guilt, hurt, anger, and inadequacy. I continued to explore and asked myself further questions.

Question: Why am I feeling these emotions?

This is about identifying why you are experiencing these emotions as opposed to others, so you understand the beliefs behind them.

My answer: I was feeling rejected, hurt, and angry because I believed Mum was judging me and having a subtle indirect dig at me. I believed she was sending me a message that she couldn't just come out and say directly, the message that I did not do enough for her compared to her friend's son. I believed that she was not seeing what I did do for her.

I felt guilty because I should be doing more for her. I should have more money, take her more places, and I felt responsible for her happiness. And because I didn't do more for her, what I did do was not enough, so I was not good enough as a daughter.

Question: What triggered it?

This is about identifying the specific external thing that triggered the internal reaction. It may have been a word, sentence, energy, situation, look, or behavior.

My answer: the words my mum used, "Tim is so wonderful to his mother. He pays for her to fly to see him regularly, and he takes her to dinner and on adventures. He is so good to his mother."

Umm, why was I interpreting what Mum said as her judging me when all she was doing was sharing what her friend's son had done? In fact, she did not even mention me.

The only way I could have interpreted my mother's words as her judging me was if I experienced this in the past before, so I asked myself . . .

Question: Where in the past have I experienced this before?

This is where you identify which layer situation this reaction comes from. There will be the original situation, the earliest one, and then there will potentially be layers in your layer—other situations that are similar that reinforced the layer.

My answer: my grandma comparing me to my brother. I was left with the feeling of not being good enough. Even though at the age of four I would fold the washing with her, scrub the copper bottoms of the pots and pans, and do everything I could around her home to help—it was never enough. Even on her deathbed, my grandma recognized my brother and not me.

So the emotions I was feeling were not about Mum and the current situation; they were about what my grandma had said and done to me in the past. This was where my rejection, guilt, hurt, anger, and feelings of inadequacy stemmed from. It was the girl in me from that situation at that age that was feeling the emotion and reaction.

I did not need to address this with Mum, as I could work with and heal the emotions myself.

I now understood what I was aware of, and I identified the reaction. I knew why I was experiencing the reaction and where it came from. I had some options as to what I could do about the emotions now that I acknowledged and understood them.

1. I could still react and take it out on Mum (dumping my issues on her).
2. I could suppress the emotion and protect myself from it, pretending it was not there (so it could surface and I could react at a later stage).
3. I could move to the next of the five steps, which is where I ACCEPT what I was aware of and have acknowledged.

Step Three: ACCEPTANCE

A friend used the term "yield" as another way of describing the third step of acceptance. It is the process of giving way to the pressure and fight, giving in and submitting.

Oh, how does this sit for you? "Ahhhhhhh," I hear you balking, "there is no way I am giving in to anyone." In fact, this is about you giving in to yourself. Giving in to what you are experiencing and processing. Giving in does not mean giving up or losing. Acceptance involves ceasing making what you are processing, thinking, and feeling wrong. It means embracing and loving yourself even when it is uncomfortable parts of yourself that you are embracing.

Acceptance and acknowledgment are sometimes defined similarly. In the five steps the process for each is very different, and it is important you implement the steps individually if you choose to heal and develop yourself.

When you accept something, you stop fighting it, you cease rejecting and making it wrong. You remove the block you have as to what you are fighting; instead, you welcome it and make it OK that it is there.

There is a physical process of relaxing into and becoming still with what you have not been accepting. There is a peacefulness in the embracing of what you are accepting. You are surrendering to yourself and what is going on for you in your mental, emotional, energy, physical, and spiritual processing. You give in to your processing and all aspects of it while remaining fully conscious of what you are doing.

You take responsibility for what you are experiencing, you take ownership of it. The experience can feel like a balloon deflating and sinking into your processing. This is so you can work with it. You give everything going on inside yourself permission to be there.

In that moment you accept what you are experiencing, and this enables you to work with your processing rather than working against it. Acceptance is what enables you to truly deal with what you are processing and move beyond it.

If you do not accept what you are experiencing, then you will be judging, rejecting, and suppressing it, so how can you work with something you are not accepting? You will reinforce the layer. This is why acceptance and you making what you are experiencing OK is so important.

Give yourself permission to be feeling what you are feeling, thinking what you are thinking, and processing what you are processing. Give yourself permission to accept what is, so you can move forward and look at your options and choices as to what you do about it.

People often share with me that they are aware of what they are experiencing emotionally and in their processing. They understand where it came from and why—the acknowledgment step. Yet they still continue to experience the same processing and outcomes. The reason is this acceptance step: they have not accepted what has happened, what the impacts were on both themselves and others, and the processing they experience. So any step they have taken to change the outcome has not been sustainable.

Acceptance requires ceasing rejecting and controlling the emotions, feelings, and thoughts within yourself that you are protecting yourself from. It involves embracing and truly feeling what you are experiencing. This can be frightening for some because in doing so, you admit and face your truth and that can be uncomfortable and painful, but in the end healing and liberating.

True change cannot happen until you accept something inside yourself. How can you heal, do something about it, and move beyond it if you do not accept it?

Acceptance Example

I wanted to fight like crazy my reaction to my mother's comment. I heard myself saying, "No, I should not be thinking this way, I can't say that to my mother, I should not be feeling this." The internal battle was fierce. Then, I paused for a moment. The most important step in acceptance was for me to make what I was feeling and thinking OK. Here's what I did to achieve this:

I focused on relaxing internally, breathing out, and watching what was happening within myself, instead of engaging in it and trying to tell myself off or battle it out. I gave into what was happening inside and said to myself, "It is OK that I am feeling this. I choose to stop making it wrong, and I surrender to, accept, and embrace my process and processing." I felt the change internally. I felt the gentleness and flow. I reminded myself that this was a gift for me to love, as I was loving myself by accepting my processing.

I could now move to the next step, which is where I would look at my options and choices about what I could do with my reaction and emotions.

Step Four: OPTIONS AND CHOICES

This is where you explore the options available to you as to how you will process out, release, and express your reaction. This is so that you can consciously influence the outcome and ensure you experience a different one to the past layer situation that your reaction stems from.

To explore your options and choices you ask yourself questions and self-facilitate, so you can explore the options available as to how you will achieve your outcome. The questions start with exploring the desired outcome.

Question: What outcome do I want?

It is really important for you to be clear on the outcome you want. This is so that your intention is clear, as this will guide your choices and actions. You also want to ensure you are aiming for a different outcome to the layer ones you previously experienced. Be very clear on what you want to achieve.

In deciding how you will respond to your internal reaction, the outcome you want to achieve should involve you processing out your emotions and reactions in a way that does not hurt you, others, or anything, and is healthy and healing for you. You want to walk away feeling good about yourself and that you did the right thing and the right thing by you.

Having identified the outcome you want, the next question explores your options.

Question: What options do I have?

I used to believe there were only two choices in every situation, and they tended to be the extremes. I discovered that I have multitudes of choices in every situation I am in. I used to spread my arms out wide and use my hands as the reference points of the extremes of the options I was seeing. I would then look at what other options were available to me, on the invisible spectrum between my hands. This was a great way of anchoring the process for expanding my awareness and getting me to look more widely at my options. You should certainly give this a try too as it may help you similarly.

Grow your ability to explore all the possible options and alternatives available to choose from in any situation. Options give you the opportunity to explore beyond the parameters of what you have previously done and for you to be creative and resourced in an array of different approaches that you can take in any given situation. Options give you choice as to how you can grow, learn, and evolve.

Having explored all your options, the final question supports you to identify the options for achieving your outcome.

Question: Which option will achieve my outcome?

From all the options you identified, the options you choose to act on should be one that achieves the new outcome you intend to experience. This enables you to make an informed choice as to your best option.

To see how to proceed with the options and choices step, let's return to the example of me and my mum.

Options and Choices Example

Question: What outcome do I want?

In my example with my mother, the outcome I wanted was to understand what my mother truly meant and also to release and process out my emotions, change the pattern of my self-talk, and express this in a healthy way where I did not hurt my mum, myself, or anyone else.

So the next question I asked myself was:

Question: What options do I have?

Option 1: I could react to Mum and dump my emotions on her, fully aware of what I was doing. I would feel guilty later as this was not the right thing to do. This would impact her and me even more, and was not fair on my mother, as she was not the issue here.

Option 2: I could suppress the emotions and self-talk inside myself, which would impact me. Then it would only surface again the next time it was triggered.

Option 3: I could say to Mum, "I just have to do something quickly. I will be back in a moment." Then I could go outside and voice out loud on my own what I was feeling and processing, and get the emotion off my chest. This process would download the energy and the reaction.

Option 4: I could say, "Mum, I just need to do something before I carry on the conversation with you." I could then go and free write my emotions and processing to download it.

Option 5: if the emotion was not overwhelming, I could say, "Hey, Mum, it is really interesting, what you just said about Lisa and Tim, I interpreted it as you judging me. I know you are not. It triggered a reaction in me from a situation from the past about Grandma . . ." and I could just talk to her about it.

And not forgetting the other part of my desired outcome— to understand what my mother meant—I would ask her what her processing was behind sharing this story with me with the intention of understanding her. This approach could be included as part of options 3, 4, and 5.

At this point, I was ready to ask myself the final question . . .

Question: Which option will achieve my outcome?

The outcome I identified for myself is that I wanted to process out the emotion and my self-talk. I wanted to release what I was processing. I wanted to understand Mum, and I did not want to hurt myself, Mum, or anyone else.

The first two options would not achieve my desired outcome. Taking it out on Mum and suppressing it in myself were not going to achieve my outcome. Any of the last three options would achieve my outcome. So, that made it choice time.

The Choice Part of Step Four

In stepping back and seeing all the options available in each situation, as well as exploring the outcome you want first before choosing an option, you are taking responsibility to consciously influence the outcomes you experience in your life.

In the scenario with me and my mum, once I was clear on the three options that would achieve my outcome, quite simply I knew I could pick one of the options, 3, 4, or 5, and implement it.

The next and final step is about pulling into action what you have been processing.

Step Five: ACTION

It is now up to you to do something different to what you have always done. For you to influence your life and the experiences you have. The fifth and final step is action. This is about you acting on the option you choose. Whichever option you do choose, implement the option that allows you to express and release your internal reaction.

You may find you do not have to take any action because when you reach the acceptance step and you surrender, your emotions dissolve, and the processing unravels at that moment. Dissolved and resolved.

Your emotions want you to give them attention and acceptance. Your emotions are attached to the layer, which has a girl or boy in you at the age the layer situation occurred. So in the emotions wanting acceptance, it is the girl or boy in you who just wants to be heard, seen, felt, and accepted.

Acceptance of self is you loving yourself.

Action Example

As I accepted the emotions and surrendered to my processing, I felt the reaction lighten and dissolve. The intensity of the energy and emotion subsided.

I chose option five, and I asked Mum, "What was your reason for sharing your story about Lisa and her son, as I was not clear on it?"

Mum explained that she shared the story because she was worried about Lisa being alone, so she was pleased that Tim, the son, gave Lisa time and attention. Mum identified with Lisa's situation.

I then shared with Mum my processing. The difference was that I was quite gentle in my approach, and there was no blame or dumping. It was mother and daughter sharing their stories. What a difference from previous times.

Outcomes

After you have taken action, responding rather than reacting, it is powerful to take time to reflect on the outcome. Recognize what you have done differently in the situation from previous times and how the outcome is different from the previous layer situation outcomes.

Acknowledge and accept not just the big differences, but all differences, no matter how big, small, significant, or insignificant they can seem. There is a difference, and that is what is important. This will assist you to continue to grow your confidence and ability to apply the five steps, respond, and create different outcomes for yourself. You can gain insight into how your process of responding rather than reacting has progressed and what the benefits are that you are gaining from your growth.

<u>Self-Facilitation Activity—Retroactive Application of the Five Steps</u>

There is great value in you revisiting situations from your past where you reacted emotionally and applying the five steps retroactively through reflection. This will resource you with insight into your layer experiences, triggers, and processing, so should the situations present themselves again, you will be conscious of the different steps you can take. Identify a number of these situations to explore retroactively with the five steps.

Free write and explore your reactions and responses to understand and process them. And where possible apply the five steps at the time you experience the reaction.

First, choose a situation from your past where you reacted emotionally. Now, apply the five steps:

a. What were the reactions you experienced internally?
- *Describe the processing you experienced, the physical feelings, sensations, and mental processing.*

b. What were the emotions attached to the internal reaction?
- *Identify the emotions attached to each of the reactions you had and describe what you experienced emotionally.*

c. Why were you feeling the emotions you experienced attached to the reaction?
- *Identify why you experienced the emotions you felt with each of your reactions. What was the reason for each emotion you felt?*

d. What triggered each of the reactions?
- *Describe what it was specifically that happened externally that triggered the reactions internally. Was it a look, a tone, a word, a statement, energy,*

a person, or a situation? It is important you identify the specifics to support you with the next question.

e. When in the past have you experienced these external triggers and internal reactions?
- *Identify the situation and layer where each trigger, reaction, and emotion comes from. Where possible, identify your age in the past situation.*

f. How did you externally express the internal reaction at the time?
- *What behavior, words, tone, expressions, and actions did you take to express your internal reactions when you experienced them?*

g. What were the outcomes you experienced as a result of your reactions?
- *What were the outcomes of the situations where you reacted externally?*

h. Accept the processing, accept the feelings.
- *Make the reaction, the emotions, and the past situation OK. Do not fight it or make it wrong. This enables you to work with what you experienced.*

i. Identify what you can do differently to express the reaction in a healthy way to achieve the outcomes you want.
- *Explore each reaction to identify what outcome you want and how you can express yourself differently in these situations, so you can create a new outcome.*

j.   Identify the options and choices you had in each of the reactionary situations to determine how you could work with your internal reaction and your external expression of the reaction differently.

k.   Choose options that achieve your outcomes and commit to working with your processing to implement and take action on the options.

Five-Step Summation

Initially, in growing your ability to implement the five steps, like any process, it will take time to consciously work with it. When you have the reactions, you may require time to explore them. You will find, though, the speed at which you apply the five steps will increase, as they become more natural to you. Then you find situations where you experience the five steps instantaneously.

The awareness and acknowledgment steps can be an intellectual process. This means you can understand the theory and concept of what you are experiencing. This will not bring about true change, as you only understand it but are not living it.

Acceptance allows you to feel, embody, and experience your processing, and this is why it is one of the most important steps of all.

It is important that when you implement the five steps, you process out your emotional and mental processing so that you know you are exploring your natural process, you are feeling it, and experiencing it.

In applying the five steps, I encourage you to implement them not just when you have reactions, but at all times of your processing. The more familiar you are with the process, the easier it will be to apply when you have an emotional reaction. The five steps will become natural to you and your process.

The five steps to responding focus on how you can work with the impacts of the layer experiences to change the processing of your reactions, so you can experience different outcomes. You may find though that the same pattern of outcome keeps unfolding; that even with all the growth in your ability to apply the five steps, it feels like the same old, same old and nothing is changing.

There are additional phases you will experience in your journey, which involve learnings, lessons, uncovering, and discovering. There is a different focus for each phase and they align with the integration process, onion model, beliefs, and reacting to responding. You can feel like you are experiencing the same learning over and over again; however, you may not recognize the reason for the pattern and the lesson you are to take from the opportunity (dare I call it that!).

The next chapter explores those learnings, lessons, uncovering, and discovering phases, how to identify the particular phase you are experiencing, and which of the tools and approaches we have been exploring to apply to that phase—with the intention of healing and dissolving your layers of the past and connecting to your jewel within.

CHAPTER 12

LESSONS, LEARNINGS, UNCOVERING, AND DISCOVERING STAGES

"Hi there, have you caught any fish?"

I pause for a moment, look up, and the thought goes through my head, "This is interesting."

The couple came on the boat fully kitted out in great sports gear (you can tell what I have been processing this morning—what clothes I wear fishing!!!). The lady has come over to talk to me. This is so cool. I do notice a feeling of me slightly standing back internally though, which is not like me.

We chat and get back to fishing.

As the day goes on, she approaches me a number of times to talk. I experience a couple of moments of distance from her because this is different for me. This is unfamiliar, nothing to do with her, everything to do with me. And I am questioning in my head, "Why are you talking to me?" as I am not used to this.

By the end of the day, I noticed internally some change happening to me. Then Alan asked me, "Have you got her contact details?"

I stopped and responded, "Why?"

"So we can catch up with them," he answered.

"Oh, of course," I reply.

So I approached this wonderfully warm Irish woman whose name is Elaine, and we swapped contact details. She reached out and gave me an amazing embracing hug goodbye, and we agreed to catch up. This was different, and I was noticing the difference.

A pattern in my life was that I was just about always the person who approached other people to make a connection, talk, and initiate contact. In fact, the day before our fishing, a woman in a cafe said to my partner, "Melinda is lovely. The fact she has taken time to talk to me and engage with me is different."

I was used to being the one that reached out, and my reasoning was that I loved people. However, there was more to it than that. There were only a couple of people in my life where it was not a one-way process, where I was the one initiating contact.

Two weeks previously, I was pondering on this and the fact that I deserved to have people approach and contact me. I discovered subconscious beliefs that were attached to my processing: "I approach and contact others because people are not interested enough in me" and "I don't deserve to have people reach out to and connect with me because they are too busy."

Well, thank you beautiful angel on the fishing trip for being part of my **learning**.

The same situation from a layer situation arose again: I was in a group of people who mainly did not know each other, and I was going to take responsibility for initiating the interaction and connecting with them. The **lesson** for me to learn was not to always do this but do something different. I did, I didn't reach out, except for a smile, and this time I got to experience a new outcome.

I had been conscious of my exploration of this process in the previous two weeks, and this was what enabled me to notice the opportunity and gift in the situation. A wake-up moment happened: I saw so clearly that the space of interaction I had with others was often fully taken up by me. There was no space for others to step into it. Then came the **uncovering**: people did want to connect with me and were interested in me. People reached out and wanted to spend time with me and talk to me. This was awesome.

Your growth process has so many dimensions to it, and there are distinct stages you will experience during the development and evolvement of yourself. These stages incorporate all the elements of your processing, the different phases of integration, and all the aspects of your onion model, as well as changing your reactions to responses. Being aware of what stage you are experiencing in situations supports you to accept the process and facilitate yourself to gain the maximum benefits for yourself so that you make a difference to yourself.

The stages you experience include:

1. Lessons
2. Learnings
3. Uncovering
4. Discovering

Lessons

"Lessons"—immediately your thoughts might be of school, and if you did not enjoy school, potentially you have a layer, so the word "lesson" may be a trigger. Maybe it triggers off a reaction filled with the impacts from the layer experience. If so, capture that memory and jot it down in your notebook or Personal Processing Workbook because it's a great opportunity for you to work with that situation and processing. This is the gift of a lesson.

A lesson is an opportunity for you to be taught something, and if you choose to, learn something. Lessons are periods of time that focus on a particular subject, situation, or process. The learnings you gain from the lesson are what you choose to take on board and apply in your life. In terms of personal growth and development, if you are experiencing a lesson, then there is something for you to learn.

Lessons are where you experience a recurrence of the layer situations from your past. And questions like "Why do I keep experiencing the same pattern of these situations?" and "Why does this keep repeating in my life?" can run through your being.

Your lessons keep repeating themselves until you get all of the learnings. They are a gift and an opportunity for you. "Whatever," I hear you say as you try to dismiss the word "opportunity."

Lessons can feel like hard work, they are frustrating, and you can feel you are going nowhere. If so, then you are fighting your process; you are fighting yourself and not accepting. Understanding why they are recurring and identifying in what way the situation is different supports you to accept the lesson and identify the opportunity that is there for you.

The past layer situations continue to occur as an opportunity for you to change the pattern of your processing and behaviors. For you to unravel the conditioning, heal your emotions, release any limiting mental processing, release your persona and protection, and cease suppressing anything in yourself. So that ultimately the situation no longer is the same because of what you have learned and applied to change it. The layer and layers have dissolved, and you are you. The lesson process occurs in **integration** phases one and two.

Phase 1: reclaiming and retrieving the memories stored in your subconscious mind.

Your memory of the layer situation in your conscious mind may be selective and only contain aspects of the experience, not the full picture. The lesson keeps reoccurring to provide you with the opportunity to remember all of it. And remember the experience as it actually was, rather than how you chose to view it. This is the process of retrieving the memories attached to the lessons.

Phase 2: healing of the mental, emotional, physical, energy, and spiritual impacts of your layers.

The layer situations and lessons continue recurring to keep triggering all the different types of processing required for healing and dissolving of the layers from your past.

My beautiful lesson that presented itself in the fishing scenario was a repeated situation from my past where most of the people did not know each other. Generally, I would be the one to step into the space, say hi, and encourage interaction in the first ten minutes. I would be the one approaching others, rather than them approaching me. I would be the one holding the responsibility for the energy of the group and the connections.

Lesson situations cease when you have all the learnings. You won't experience the situation again, or if you do, you won't have an emotional attachment to the outcome, so you will see, feel, and respond to the situation differently.

Embrace the lessons as they have wonderful learning opportunities within them. Identify areas for healing and where you can take your personal power back and change the pattern of situations you don't deserve in your life anymore.

Learnings

Learnings are what you can acquire from the experience of the lessons. You can develop your awareness, understanding, acceptance, skills, knowledge, ability to respond, healing, and change in processing.

You will experience the learnings if you are open to seeing them, willing to embrace them and are committed to applying what you have learnt. Otherwise, don't bother. If you are not open to getting the learning, you are welcome to continue to experience the situations from the layers of your past, again and again. And you are the one responsible for this happening.

Learnings take many forms, and they change and transform depending on where you are at in your process of developing and what you are focusing on.

My focus on people approaching and connecting with me was something I initiated two weeks before the fishing trip. I identified some limiting beliefs and behaviors, worked with releasing them, and committed to staying open to opportunities for people to step into and approach me to connect. I let it go to allow the process to naturally unfold. When the lady approached me in the fishing situation, my initial internal feelings of standing back were because I was not fully aware of and tuned into the lesson and learning. As I trusted myself and the process, I was aware enough to embrace the process that was happening.

The learnings that accompany your lessons have processing in the form of layer impacts attached to them.

They can feel like hard work and repetitive at times. And when the lesson comes back around again, and you believe you have already got the learning, you are likely to hear yourself saying, "I have learned this already" or "I thought I had dealt with this."

Warning sign—be aware that in making these statements, you are closing yourself off from any residual and remaining healing and processing attached to the lesson. You will suppress and resist your process. You have an expectation.

I encourage you to say, "I have dealt with (or learnt) this as much as I am aware of up to this point." This will support you to stay open to embracing what may appear to be repetitive situations that may occur, so you can see why they are happening again and in what way you and they are different. This will support you to work with the learning effectively.

You will only be given what you can handle, and you will experience the lesson for as long as there is something for you to learn in the situation. The experiences will continue until the unravelling of conditioning and healing of the emotion and other impacts from the layer are completed. Until you have changed your approach to the situation, released any limiting beliefs and self-talk, and experienced different outcomes in how you feel and what you experience, the situations will continue to occur.

When you experience a recurring situation, implement the important step in the five steps, step number three—acceptance. Accept it is happening, know that this is a natural part of the process of personal growth and development, and identify the reason why it is happening. Identify the learning that you still can gain from the opportunity of the lesson. Make sure you gain the maximum benefits from the situation.

The layer situations and lessons repeat for an array of reasons:

1. You did not get the lesson and did not learn from the situation the first time. You did nothing.

- *In this situation, you will find you are unaware of what is happening in you, for you, and to you. You will also potentially feel you do not have any influence over what happens in your life, that you are a victim of circumstance and at the mercy of others.*

2. You intellectualized the lesson and learning. You understood it, you got the concept, but you did not embrace and integrate the learning. You experienced it in your head but did not feel or fully process it in your being.

- *William, a young man who had read a lot about personal development, attended my program. William identified that he was self-sabotaging. Each job he had he did something that resulted in losing his job. When he was younger, his mother did everything for him, including getting jobs for him. William grew up not fully knowing how to do things for himself or having the confidence to do so. He identified what he was doing to himself, and he recognized actions he could take to change his sabotage. At William's next job, he rang me from a cupboard that he had locked himself in. He explained to me that he was sabotaging his work situation again and could not find the confidence and strength in himself to take action to cease doing so. He had the tools; however, he had not taken a step yet to truly feeling and working with the impacts of his childhood and integrating the learnings. William lost his job again.*

3. You understood and integrated the learning internally; however, you did nothing to change the external outcome because you did not act on the internal changes.

4. The layer has many layers in it. The lesson has many learnings in it. You learned from the lesson the first time and now are ready to see and address the other learnings in the lesson.

- *The lesson from my fishing situation originated from situations where there were lots of people who did not know each other and I would not initiate anything, as I was scared of rejection. In this way, I made very few connections. One of my learnings was to change this pattern of interaction. For a number of years, I was the one who was comfortable with approaching people and connecting with them. The original learning was not to sit back and reject myself. Other learning layers of the layer were to step out, experience, and connect with others. I did this, I experienced some rejection, and it hurt. I also experienced growth in my confidence in approaching others. And as it grew, I also learned that if people did reject me, it was not about me.*

5. The situation and lesson you gain the learning from has another doorway to it. This is so you journey down another pathway of learning because you are ready to do so.

6. Your lack of self-worth impacted you in that you believed you didn't deserve to have gotten the learning in the first place. So what you do is continue to manifest the situation over and over again. Either to punish yourself or because you believe you deserve to experience the learning many times and for it to be hard work for you to get it. Enough already.

- *Oh, how many times I did this with employees: I experienced a few employees abandon their employment with my business. I learned the lesson and changed the pattern of how I managed myself and the situation. And yet in the final years of the business, there was one more employee. One that I supported after he abandoned us in that I accepted him returning to the business, and then he abandoned us again. OMG, I got it, I got it. I just needed to remind myself of the learning.*

7. The situation arises again for you to develop more options as to how you can respond in the situation. You have healed the emotional and mental

processing, grown your ability to respond, and now you have different options to choose from as to what you can do. Experiencing the lesson situation again provides you with a further opportunity for learning, so you can develop more options as to the approaches you can consciously take in any situation. And you continue to develop your ability to influence your life powerfully in the outcomes you experience.

- *My love of participants who expressed reactions to me—as I have shared, when participants go fishing to get a reaction from me, I have a number of different approaches I can choose from. I have reacted, I have sat silently and listened with nothing to say, I have asked people to leave the course, and I have responded by asking, "What sort of reaction would you like from me, I am happy to oblige?" I discovered another one to add to my list of options.*

I was delivering a work readiness program and Joseph, a young man full of talent, wisdom, and energy, who was very expressive, was in the group. His behaviors often reminded me of how I had been, and I was aware of this. There were a number of times he reacted to me and threw comments out to bait me. I acted on each of the different options I had available, including reacting. Then one day, after Joseph had gone at me, I identified at that moment another option I had. I knew I was repeating the lesson opportunity again, so the question was why, what is the learning here? And the answer presented itself, and I responded to the young man. I was very still inside, feeling grounded and gentle, and I quietly said to him, "I did not deserve to be treated that way." That was all.

Joseph went out of the room, then came back a while later and apologized. He acknowledged that his anger was at himself, not me, and that he felt safe with me, which was different for him, and that was why he reacted. Joseph had been rejecting the fact that someone cared about him, as he did not trust or believe this.

8. The lesson experience occurs again for you to acknowledge your growth. For you to recognize and see that you have learned you are doing things differently and how you have changed. This is important for you to know and own so that you have evidence of the changes in yourself and your life. So that you build your confidence in moving forward with you taking your personal power back and being more true to yourself. The key is to own all the changes you make and that occur, no matter how subtle or significant they are.

9. Then you experience the learning again so that you can consciously say to yourself, "I have learned everything I am aware of up to this point in this situation." This reflects your acceptance of the experience and leaves you open to the possibility that the situation may arise again in a different way if there is still something for you to gain from it. Then

you won't resist the process; rather you will accept it and embrace it.

You experience the lessons and learnings stages when you are:

- Processing the areas that make up the layers from your past, on the onion model. The lessons are embedded in the layers of conditioned behaviors, emotions, and underlying issues.
- Working with integration phase two: the learnings involve healing of the mental, emotional, physical, energy, and spiritual impacts of your layers.
- Identifying and releasing limiting beliefs is part of the learning process. Where you identify what is holding you back from what you truly deserve and you create new beliefs.
- Moving from reacting to responding and changing the outcomes you experience in your life. The lessons are opportunities to identify the same situations and reactions, and the learnings are opportunities to respond.
- Implementing the five steps, as you consciously work with truly embodying and effectively processing the lesson and learnings.
- Developing your self-belief and self-worth in seeing and hearing the steps, changes, and growth you have achieved from the learnings and how the lessons are different. This builds your trust and self-confidence and assists you to be clearer on what you do deserve.

Rest stop: growing your awareness of when lessons present themselves will enable you to actively embrace the learnings from the experience to gain the maximum benefit from the situation. The following self-facilitation activity is an opportunity for you to retroactively explore some of the lessons and learnings you have experienced, so you grow your awareness.

Self-Facilitation Activity—Lessons and Learnings

As with the self-facilitation activity in chapter 11, More on the Five Steps, there is value in you revisiting experiences from your past to grow your ability to be aware of and understand those situations, your processing, and your approaches in those situations. This is so if the situation arises again, you can consciously embrace the opportunities being presented and influence the outcomes for your benefit. Specifically I designed this activity to help you grow your ability to identify lesson situations and the learnings they offer.

In your notebook or Personal Processing Workbook, spend time free writing your responses to each of the following. *Utilize the above list of types of learnings to assist you with your exploration.*

> a. What are the lesson situations attached to your layer experiences that have been repetitious in your life?
> b. What are the learnings that you have gained from these situations?
> c. Is there anything for you still to learn from these situations/lessons? If so, what?

d. What has prevented you from identifying and embracing the learnings from your lessons?

e. What is it in you that has enabled you to learn from your lessons?

As you embrace your lessons and learnings, and unravel and heal, you create space for uncovering. Uncovering elements of yourself.

Uncovering

In chapter 4, The Creation of Your Layers, I suggested that you find a photo or a picture in your head of yourself as a child where you remember the amazing qualities in yourself, where you felt everything was right and safe, where you trusted yourself, and where you were you. The picture or photo provides you with a visual recollection of these qualities and supports you in reconnecting to these parts of yourself. *Did you action this?*

Uncovering is the process of removing the cover from the natural, true, and beautiful aspects of yourself that you have hidden and disconnected from. And shining the light on them, so you see them, feel them, own them, and integrate them through being conscious of those beautiful aspects of yourself and their processing. This is where the photo or picture in your head can assist you.

In terms of your personal growth and development, uncovering is removing and dissolving the protection and suppression from the wonderful and amazing parts of yourself that you have known before. From that time when you were connected to aspects of yourself before the layer situations and where you covered up that connection. In this process, you are reconnecting with yourself and elements of the true you.

When I did not fill the space of interaction, when I arrived on the fishing boat, I got to uncover parts of me I once knew and had not reconnected to. What this beautiful lady supported me to do was to experience what it was like to have others want to meet me, talk to me, and be connected to me. The last time I remember this feeling was a surprise birthday and I did not know how to handle the attention. This time I remembered the experience as a child, people wanting to be friends, and it felt so beautiful, free, simple, pure, and natural, and I accepted it. I found this in me again.

You will experience the stage of uncovering in the integration phases one and three.

Phase 1: reclaiming and retrieving the memories stored in your subconscious mind.

The memories that relate to the stage of uncovering are your wonderful ones. Memories you bring forward to your conscious mind where you remember being who you truly are, where you accessed and expressed the amazing qualities that make you you and where you trusted yourself. By bringing them to your conscious mind, you uncover what you already know and are.

Phase 3: being conscious of retrieving, reclaiming, and embracing your jewel, your amazing qualities, your knowing, your truth, and the real you.

The conscious memories you have of being still inside, feeling strong, having clarity, being grounded and gentle as a child are real, and the reason you can feel them now is that you have uncovered them and are reconnecting to these parts of yourself. The uncovering stage is where you have a conscious memory of when you expressed and experienced your amazing qualities, your jewel, your trust of yourself, being connected to your knowing, truth, and the real you. The memories will include pictures, words, feelings, and sensations. You know these elements are you because you remember and feel them. You know.

An uncovering stage I remember experiencing was when a lady said to me, "You are kind," and in my mind I was like "Hello, I don't remember anyone ever telling me this." In fact, it felt a tad foreign and very unfamiliar.

So I asked the lady, "What did I do to leave you feeling I am kind?" She shared it was the look in my eyes, my listening, and my approach. I got to see me through her eyes, which assisted me in reclaiming memories from the depths of my subconscious. Suddenly I saw the times I'd sat with my grandfather listening to him intently with curiosity and interest, looking after animals with tenderness, being gentle, and feeling so much love in offering to assist my grandfather. I could see and feel this beautiful quality in myself flooding the cells of my body.

As you uncover you, your self-belief grows. You own the amazing qualities that make you who you are. You trust yourself and your knowing. You grow your self-worth as you action what you do deserve and cease doing and accepting things you don't deserve. You value you, you make you important, and you stop blocking and sabotaging the good things in your life.

In healing your layers, you create space and are able to reconnect to the connection you once had to these parts of yourself. You uncover what you covered up with protection, suppression, personas, and layers. You allow yourself to embrace, own, and be you again.

You allow the light within you that you dimmed to shine again, both within and out of yourself. Then you come to discover there is even more to you than you remember or know.

Discovering

The stage of discovering is where you find out for the first time your many different dimensions, qualities, abilities, and expressions that you never knew you were or had. You are your own explorer of you, discovering uncharted, unknown parts of yourself.

As the healing and dissolving of the layers continue, there is more space for the parts of you that you have uncovered to be expressed and to shine in ways you have not known before. Your potential shines, grows, evolves, and you allow yourself to be all of who you truly are.

There will be qualities, attributes, potential, ability, processing in you that you have no conscious memory of. You don't remember being connected to these parts of yourself.

In discovering, you connect to the qualities and attributes in yourself that you never knew. You connect to processing, capabilities, and talents you have never known to be there because your layers prevented you from reaching the age or stage to express them.

I never knew I had an ability to understand and connect to people's processing in the way I do. Discovering this has been so buzzy in that I love it and it fascinates me.

As your self-belief grows, your trust in yourself and the process of your life supports you to open up to endless possibilities and opportunities.

As your self-worth grows, your valuing of yourself, your deservedness, and your energy become more open to receiving more love, abundance, and everything else life has to offer.

The discovering process is a limitless space, where anything is possible.

You get out of the way of your soul and process, and give yourself permission to be and express who you truly are and what is possible. You discover and connect with yourself. You are inspired by who you truly are, and you allow you to express you. You and your jewel within are one and the same. You are your true you. You are your jewel.

Rest stop: reclaiming, reconnecting to yourself, and owning yourself, the true you and all the wonderful aspects, abilities, qualities, and elements of yourself—that is the focus of the following self-facilitation activity. It provides an opportunity for you to take time to be conscious of what you have uncovered and are uncovering and discovering in and about yourself.

Self-Facilitation Activity—Uncovering and Discovering

In your notebook or Personal Processing Workbook, spend time free writing your responses to each of the following.

a. What are the beautiful and amazing aspects of yourself that you have uncovered? Consider both prior to reading this book and since you have been reading it.

b. What are the memories attached to what you have uncovered in yourself?

c. What are the beautiful and amazing aspects of yourself that you have discovered? Consider abilities, interests, qualities, and attributes.

d. How does uncovering and discovering these aspects of yourself influence how you feel and how you live your life?

The following chapter is the final one of your adventure with this book. It provides an opportunity to reflect on where you have travelled in yourself, what you have experienced, and what you have learned and uncovered on the way. Your adventure of unravelling, healing, and dissolving your layers and the reclaiming of yourself will continue.

CHAPTER 13

YOU MAKE A DIFFERENCE TO YOUR LIFE

I am bathing in the reflection of the amazing process that has evolved and the changes that have happened since the unravelling of my limiting belief, "I don't have many friends" that I worked with in chapter 8. Little did I know that when I replaced this limiting belief with two new helpful beliefs, "I choose to accept the people in my life are the ones that are meant to be in my life now" and "I choose to be open to more wonderful people in my life," that such magic would unfold. Beautiful friends from my past have returned to my life, and interactions with previous participants have transpired. New connections have been created and friendships developed with people throughout the world, outside of my world. And new experiences where people I didn't know approached me, instead of me being the initiator. I am looking through different eyes, feeling differently about myself. I know I am generating and emitting a different approach and energy.

As I ponder on these experiences a warm feeling floods my being and a smile forms on my face. Then a thought comes to mind, "I am the person who generally initiates contact with my friends, rather than them contacting me." This is not an unfamiliar thought; however, this time I have no reaction, no emotion or any other processing that is impacting, except the thought. This trend of interaction has been a bone of contention for years, resulting in me feeling rejected, not being important, and all the other processing that goes with it. This time—none of that. There is a fascination and a curiosity to understand why, to explore my process, gain insight, and check if there is anything limiting or holding me back in the growth of me.

So rather than reacting, shutting down, or becoming accusatory with my friends, I take steps to gain insight into their processes to see and explore how this pattern has evolved. I email a friend, Jaime, explaining that I want to understand my processing and explore why our contact tends to be mainly initiated by me. What a magical and loving process that unfolds. Jaime shares that she doesn't contact me, as she doesn't want our friendship to only be about her processing or her issues even though she knows that I would gladly listen to her. Her caring and consideration are beautiful, and I encourage her, "Just ask me."

Through our processing together, Jaime discovers that she is the one who initiates most of the contact with her other friends. And when she does contact them, she hears their issues and people don't often ask her how she is and she is worried she does the same to me.

In working with my limiting belief about friends, I worked on healing the feelings of being rejected by people, ceasing rejecting myself, and filling my neediness to belong by belonging in me. I identified the limiting beliefs I could release and change, and unraveled the pattern of conditioning of contacting my friends to find I was left with me and the beautiful curiosity of wanting to understand.

I then asked questions with pure intent to understand the truth around my friend's processing, rather than my interpretation of it. And she also gained insight from the conversation, which has enabled our friendship to become more real and free. This was made possible by a want on my part to take action to make a difference to myself. These processes and the magic that comes from them are amazing.

As this is the last chapter of this first I Make a Difference book, I am sharing this powerful example from my life to show you what is possible and so that you feel the energy and see the magic that happens when you commit to taking action to make a difference to yourself.

Similar to the reflections I've shared about my working through the I Make a Difference process that unfolded from this one limiting belief, it is important that you take time to acknowledge each step you've taken and each change you've made over your course of reading and reflecting in your journey through this book, no matter how subtle or massive It may seem. The purpose of this is so that you have evidence of your progress and the difference you are making to yourself and your life. The more you see the differences, the more your confidence and trust of yourself and your process develops. The more you focus on how things are currently, rather than how you used to see them. So, here is an opportunity for you to embrace the differences you have experienced from your adventure.

Pause, Process and Explore: Recognizing Your Differences

At the end of the first chapter, you spent time exploring and identifying your responses to the following questions:

a. What drew you to read this book?

b. What are the questions you have that you want to find answers to?

c. What areas in yourself do you want to learn about, explore, change, grow, and/or develop? And why?

d. What else would you like to achieve or gain from reading this book?

Go back to what you wrote in response to these questions. This is where you began your I Make a Difference adventure in reading this book. Read what you wrote and explore where you have come to now.

From what you wrote then to where you are now, write responses to the following questions:

e. What have you learned and discovered about yourself?

f. What questions have you had answered?

g. What aspects of yourself do you still have questions about?

h. What aspects of yourself do you still want to address, develop, and change?

i. What areas of yourself have come to your attention that you didn't know or think about prior to reading the book that you want to work with and explore further?

From here, respond to the following questions:

j. What key aspects of yourself do you commit to working with to make a difference to you?
k. What steps and action will you take to work with these parts of yourself?
l. What are the commitments you are making to yourself?

Know that the healing and unravelling you are doing does make a difference and takes you down pathways that bring about beautiful experiences—as I described happened for me and so many other IMAD program participants—as your internal world opens up to the true you and your external world opens up to what you deserve.

It requires your want, commitment, involvement, and ability to take action. As well as you developing your willingness to receiving the gifts of change and difference flowing your way and the willingness to ask questions to understand. And the ability to see all the changes and wonderful things that are unfolding within yourself and in how you express yourself externally, in situations, in how others interact with you, and the changes in how you are seeing and hearing others.

Recap: Tools and Approaches So I Make a Difference

As you expand your awareness, gain more insight and utilize the tools and approaches to develop yourself, your ability to heal the impacts of your past and dissolve your layers enhances so that you bring about change and do things differently. Do so, first and foremost for yourself, and then the change will be real and sustainable.

You have all the experiences and knowledge from your life to support you as well as the I Make a Difference tools and approaches to assist you in your process of healing, growing, and reclaiming yourself. To recap these are the tools and approaches you can apply and integrate into how you live your life:

- Free writing to download and let go of what you are processing and experiencing
- Self-facilitation for self-exploration
- Identifying and working with your mental, emotional, physical, energy, and spiritual processes
- The I Make a Difference Onion Model
- The three phases of integration with yourself
- Your beliefs: identifying and growing your helpful ones; working with the limiting ones to identify their origins, release them, and create new helpful ones
- Growing your ability to respond rather than react
- Working with the five steps of responding to assist with your self-understanding, self-acceptance, and self-development
- Identifying and working with your lessons, learnings, uncovering, and discovering stages of growth

The process of unravelling, healing, and dissolving is in your hands. It will be uncomfortable at times, also joyous and wonderful. It will keep changing, and the times of discomfort will become less and more joyous times will ensue.

Only you can put these into action. It's up to you.

Experience the Difference. Be the Difference

In honoring what you have explored, the growth you have experienced, there are two final questions for you to explore.

- How willing and how committed are you to going to and owning your truth and truly healing and reclaiming yourself?
- How willing and committed are you to being who you were truly born as and are?

Whatever your answers, in reading this book you will be more true to yourself and will have made a lasting difference to yourself. Each word you have read, whether you are conscious of it or not, will have seeped into your subconscious mind. When you are ready to or if you are meant to, the words and processes will be in your conscious mind at the time you need to work with them.

You cannot go backwards from what you have explored in the book or experienced in your life. You have exposed yourself to more of your truth and the truth always surfaces. You can only go forward, deeper, and broader in your awareness, understanding, healing, reclaiming, and developing ot yourself.

If you choose to continue the adventure through the next legs of the journey of the collection of I Make a Difference books, you will explore more of yourself. You will be immersed in other processes that will assist in your understanding, reclaiming, and developing of yourself.

In the meantime, what is important is to focus on the now and the true you—that time you remember when everything in your world and yourself was right, free, and filled with curiosity, wonder, and awe—keep connecting to that part of yourself. When you do, look at the world around you through those eyes, those senses, and from that place within yourself.

Get out of the way of your soul, your truth, the truth, and yourself.

Trust yourself and your answers within. Have faith in your ability to discover, reclaim, and be you.

You can have the peacefulness, you can feel love in its pure form, you can be you. And only you can give yourself permission to be the real you.

You can heal your emotions, you can respond to life, you can reclaim all the amazing parts of yourself, and you can be the unique and natural you.

The light and answers are within you for you to return home to yourself.

You are the jewel that is within you.

I encourage you to connect with me with questions, to share stories, or to learn how we could work together in your journey: *melinda@imakeadifferenceimad.com* **and** *www.imakeadifferenceimad.com*.

I send lots of fantabulous energy, magical experiences, and self-belief your way.

PLEASE SHARE WITH ME YOUR FEEDBACK AND PROCESSING FROM READING THE BOOK

Thank you for taking the step in reading my book, going on the I Make a Difference adventure, and, most importantly—valuing and loving yourself by doing so.

I value and love receiving feedback about individual's experiences with I Make a Difference. I would love to have your input. It will help in the further growth and development—both of myself, personally, and my future books. Also, in sharing with me your experience with I Make a Difference, I can enhance the value of the experiences for more readers.

Please leave me an **honest review on the market place you purchased from**, so I can understand your processing and experience of the book.

Thank you, thank you, thank you—for believing in and caring about yourself, for making a difference to yourself.

—Melinda Cates

EXPLORE OPPORTUNITIES TO MAKE A DIFFERENCE TO YOU!
CONTACT MELINDA TODAY!

Are you interested in receiving notifications when my next books are available?

Do you want to learn more about one-on-one personal processing sessions?

Would you like to discuss options for organizing an I Make a Difference Personal Development program in your area?

Do you want to explore something else related to I Make a Difference?

Please contact me!

- Email me — *melinda@imakeadifferenceimad.com*
- Visit — *www.imakeadifferenceimad.com*

ABOUT THE I MAKE A DIFFERENCE BOOK COLLECTION

The four books in the I Make a Difference collection offer an unfolding process that follows the I Make a Difference Onion Model structure introduced in book one. They guide you in a natural way, so you continue to develop your awareness, understanding, and acceptance of yourself, during the process of unravelling, healing, reclaiming, and discovering you, the true you.

I Make a Difference—Book 1
Dissolve and Heal the Layers from Your Past and Discover the Jewel Within

In opening this first book, you are embarking on the I Make a Difference adventure, opening yourself to the exploration of you—your mental, emotional, energy, and physical processing. This book, which introduces the I Make a Difference Onion Model structure, will support you on this self-exploration, so you can develop your ability to be self-reliant in making an internal difference to yourself.

I Make a Difference—Book 2
Unravel the Conditioned Behaviors that Suppress Who You Are

Your adventure continues in book two. It brings into focus the conditioned behaviors, approaches, and processes that keep the layers of your past preserved. Additionally it addresses your limiting and impacting ways that suppress your emotions, your magical and amazing attributes, your truth, and the light of your jewel within.

Book two provides you the resources to unravel and dissolve these controlling, fear-based, and untrusting aspects of your behavior, so that you can reclaim more of who you truly are.

I Make a Difference—Book 3
Accept, Love, and Heal Your Emotions

Book three continues your adventure as you deep dive into your layers, the layers in the layers and into your emotions. This leg of your journey focuses on growing your ability to identify and distinguish the emotions you are feeling, the process attached to them, and their origins, so you can learn to accept, love, and heal them.

As you heal your emotions, you cease your reactionary behaviors, you release your emotional attachment to people, situations, and outcomes, and you take back responsibility for your emotional well-being. You take further steps to becoming self-reliant in self-facilitating your own processing and creating outcomes that are right and true for you.

I Make a Difference—Book 4
Dissolve the Final Layer Remnants to Be the Jewel Within

The last bastion, the last line of defense and protection from you truly being you, so you can reclaim your personal power, your choices, your life, and be the true you.

Book four is the dissolving of the last remaining elements of your layers—the "underlying issues." In your conditioned behaviors and suppressed emotions lurk these underlying issues. They are the fundamental ways in how you view and treat yourself, the emotional conclusions and impacts stemming from your experience of the layer situations and how you were treated. In healing these remaining areas, you are left with one place to connect to, reclaim, accept, and be—the jewel within you.

The subtitles of books two to four are subject to change.

ACKNOWLEDGMENTS

Dougal, my dear friend and colleague—thank you for the sharing of a belief that we could create our own unique way of facilitating. For your belief in me, for the D of MAD and for the MAD of IMAD. Without you IMAD, GMAD, and CMAD would not have gotten their names. You taught me so much with regards to training, and you helped me to develop my unique way of facilitating. I am only sorry you do not get to read this book, as you were the one who first said that I would write the book. I am sorry I only found out you had passed while writing this book. I love you, my friend. Thank you from every part of my being.

Nancy Pile, my amazing editor who I view as a friend—you gave me the greatest gift in my experience of writing my book—the discovery of more of me. You are an angel that was and is invested, I knew and felt this. Thank you from my soul for your truth, your care, for being you, for getting it, and for what you have done for me, for I Make a Difference, for this book, and for the people who will read it.

Racheal Cox—thank you for formatting my book, your understanding, your care, your communication and for bringing my book visually to life.

Nina Kate Design—thank you for taking my book cover design, putting the touches on it only you can do and bringing it to life and making it real for me.

Every participant that has attended and completed the I Make a Difference program—thank you for being willing to take the step to trust yourself, me, and the IMAD program to make a difference to yourselves. For the sharing and for allowing me to see you, you added to the depth of what I share.

My beautiful and treasured friends, **Katherine and Barb**—you walked beside me when I was so vulnerable. You shared your truth with me. You put your angel wings around me when I needed it. You reflected back to me who I really was. You have loved me unconditionally. Thank you for seeing me.

Clare, my friend—your belief, your integrity, your honoring, and your feedback have supported my way forward. Thank you for your commitment to yourself and to the IMAD process.

Lise—thank you for valuable guidance, sharing, friendship, excitement, and helping me to make this happen.

Leanne—my amazing cousin, your love, your words of encouragement helped me believe I could do this.

Miranda—thank you for your input, your support, your enthusiasm, your processing, and your questions.

Jess, Edwin, Deb, and Natalia—thank you for the feedback you gave me about myself, which supported me to see myself through your eyes, which helped me believe this was possible.

Sarah—your sharing, your likes, you being there, and your laughter have added to what I have been able to do. You have been my pompom girl, and I love you so much for that.

Kowhai, my friend—thank you for your clarity, your receptivity, and the insightful feedback you shared. For our walks, our talks, our processing and growth, which supported me in the steps I have taken with the book and the websites.

Dayna—there were moments when I was frustrated and feeling self-doubt and your excitement and enthusiasm for my book, made a difference to me. Thank you for being there.

To the **beta readers, Lynne, Emma, Lauren, Yvie, Jaime, Rod, Barbara, Clare, and Lise**—you provided feedback that added huge value to the process of the book. Thank you.

Jaimie—for embracing the chapters and diving into your processing in applying the processes and approaches, and the amazing and incredible growth you have done and continue to do. Thank you for your spiritual love and being my friend.

Lynne—for opening yourself to yours and the I Make a Difference process, and in providing me with the feedback and evidence of what I knew possible in reading the book.

Angela—thank you for being a beautiful human being and Astrologer that provided the feedback I needed at the right time that resulted in me designing the IMAD program.

Hamish—thank you for not just being an amazing Astrologer, for being a friend, for your sharing and for encouraging my writing and reflecting back what my knowing knew.

Paul, my friend—you have stood by me in rough times, and you saw and shared with me what you knew I could do. You have always believed in me, even during the times of you not being very well.

Trevor—my protective, supportive and consistent friend. You have been there with me through so much, we have laughed, cried, danced and paddled through a lot, even though it was an interesting introduction. Thank you.

Mere—you were a big part of this journey at so many levels. Thank you for the love, your support, for walking with me through so many amazing and painful experiences, for the difference we facilitated with so many people, and for being such a significant part of my healing.

To my brother **Johnny**—through our relationship I have learned so much about myself and the conditioned dynamics of family. If I had not experienced this, I would not have the added insight I have. Love you

My father—thank you for all the experiences I had with you that enabled me to relate to so many people.

To **my cats**—thank you for disturbing me regularly, so I took a break, and for keeping me company and lying on my desk (and sometimes my keyboard) while I wrote.

Thank you—**ME**—I did it.

ABOUT THE AUTHOR

Hi, I'm Melinda, my formative life experiences impacted me in that I hated who I was, however I knew there was more to me, something that was precious inside me, that I could not connect to so how could anyone else. So I spent most of my life studying myself and discovering the answers, tools, and processes within myself, so I could find and become me, the true me. I spent years immersed in my own self development, and in developing my own way of self-facilitating and facilitating others. I designed the I Make a Difference (IMAD) Personal Development Program in 2000, the I Make a Difference Onion Model being the foundation of the process.

For over fifteen years I have facilitated and walked beside thousands of individuals in business, in the Department of Corrections, disengaged youth, individuals with disabilities and workplace injuries, migrants and refugees, traditional owners the Aboriginal people of Australia, long term unemployed and members of the general public who have made a difference to themselves, their families, their workplace, their communities and their lives.

To learn more about me and the I Make a Difference books, the I Make a Difference Personal Development Program, workshops, and one on-one personal processing sessions, please check out my website www.imakeadifferenceimad.com—or send me an email melinda@imakeadifferenceimad.com.

My greatest joy is helping others to explore and work through their processing, and find their true selves to live a life of groundedness, freedom, gentleness, and strength.